INSTRUCTOR'S MANUAL AND TEST BANK

Your College Experience
Strategies for Success

Seventh Edition

John N. Gardner
University of South Carolina, Columbia

A. Jerome Jewler
University of South Carolina, Columbia

Betsy O. Barefoot
Policy Center on the First Year of College

Prepared by
Suzanne L. Hamid
Lee University

THOMSON
━━━✦━━━ ™
WADSWORTH

Australia • Brazil • Canada • Mexico • Singapore • Spain • United Kingdom • United States

THOMSON
WADSWORTH

Instructor's Manual and Test Bank
Your College Experience: Strategies for Success, **Seventh Edition**
Gardner/Jewler/Barefoot
Prepared by Suzanne L. Hamid

Executive Editor: *Carolyn Merrill*
Development Editor: *Cathy Murphy*
Assistant Editor: *Eden Kram*
Technology Project Manager: *Joe Gallagher*

Senior Project Manager, Editorial Production: *Samantha Ross*
Senior Print Buyer: *Mary Beth Hennebury*
Printer: *West Group*

Printed in the United States of America

1 2 3 4 5 6 7 09 08 07 06

ISBN 1-4130-2067-4

Thomson Higher Education
25 Thomson Place
Boston, MA 02210-1202
USA

For more information about our products, contact us at:
Thomson Learning Academic Resource Center
1-800-423-0563

For permission to use material from this text or product, submit a request online at
http://www.thomsonrights.com
Any additional questions about permissions can be submitted by e-mail to **thomsonrights@thomson.com**

Contents

Part 1: Plan Ahead

Part 2: Take Charge of Learning

Part 3: Sharpen Your Skills

Part 4: Get Connected

Part 5: Know Yourself

Introduction

Welcome to the Instructor's Manual and Test Bank for Gardner, Jewler and Barefoot's *Your College Experience: Strategies for Success,* Seventh Edition. The contributors who assisted in writing this manual have drawn from their expertise and experience in the classroom. Here is what this rich resource has to offer:

A. Chapter Objectives
Objectives clarify the main points of each chapter and what is most important to communicate to first-year students in the teaching of that chapter.

B. Timing of Chapter Coverage
This gives an indication of when it is most useful to assign a chapter and suggests links to other relevant chapters that can be taught in conjunction.

C. About the Topics in this Chapter
Experts in their fields give suggestions on how to best present the material in each chapter.

D. Suggested Outline for Addressing Topics in the Chapter
The outlines offer a three-step plan for each session, weaving in items such as lecture launchers, chapter exercises, group activities, peer leader assistance, case studies, and more.

E. Test Questions
There are over twenty objective questions (true/false, short answer, multiple choice) that can be copied directly from this manual and used in the classroom. Answer keys are included. Each chapter also includes essay questions that can be used as the basis for writing activities.

F. Web Resources
Helpful web links and additional resources complement each topic.

Additional Teaching Aids for Instructors

Toll-Free Consultation Service
1-800-400-7609 is a special toll-free consultation phone line dedicated to help instructors of first year students and provide information on Thomson Wadsworth products and services.

Custom Publishing Options
Faculty can select chapters from this and other Thomson Wadsworth College Success titles to bind with their own materials into a fully customized book. For more information, contact your Thomson Wadsworth representative or visit http://success.wadsworth.com.

Unbound Version of *Your College Experience*
Students can easily create their own course-specific binder using this three-hole punch version of the text. This allows students to create their own customized reference guide by adding material how and when they choose. ISBN 1-4130-2071-2

ExamView® Computerized Test Bank for *Your College Experience*
ExamView is a premiere test-building program that allows instructors to quickly create tests and quizzes customized to individual courses. ExamView's *Quick Test Wizard* guides you step-by-step through the process of creating and printing a test in minutes. Tests can contain up to 250 questions using 12 unique question types. ISBN 1-4130-2068-2

iLrn™ College Success
An integrated testing, tutorial, and class management system that is as powerful as it is easy to use. iLrn correlates self-assessments, electronic journals that encourage students to reflect on their progress, essay questions and exercises, and "Test Your Knowledge" interactive quizzes to each of the chapters in this text. Pin-coded and web-based, iLrn College Success replaces the CD-ROM that accompanied previous editions of this book.

College Success Factors Index
This unique online assessment tool allows students to easily identify the behaviors and attitudes that will help them succeed in college. Instructors can use this tool to track students' progress in the course. The index is housed on the iLrn College Success website.

Multimedia Manager 2007
Our Multimedia Manager for College Success makes classroom preparation a snap. With content that is easy to customize, this one-step presentation tool makes course preparation faster and simpler—and lectures more engaging. FREE to qualified adopters and organized by 14 common college success topics, the Multimedia Manager helps you assemble, edit, and present tailored multimedia lectures for your course. We have updated the Multimedia Manager with new Microsoft® PowerPoint® presentations, new video clips, new images, and new web links that can supplement your College Success Course.

JoinIn™ on TurningPoint®
Transform any lecture into an interactive experience for students with JoinIn™ on TurningPoint® software – our multimedia content created specifically for use with personal response systems. Combined with your choice of several leading keypad systems, JoinIn™ turns an ordinary PowerPoint application into powerful audience response software. With just a click on a hand-held device, your students can immediately respond to multiple-choice questions, polls, and interactive exercises. Available to qualified college and university adopters.

Turnitin®
A revolutionary plagiarism tool that allows you, the instructor, to check every student's paper for plagiarism against documents on the internet, books, and journals in the ProQuest database, and over 10 million papers already submitted. Students use the Internet to submit their paper and the instructor receives an originality report in a short time. Ensure your students' papers are original works.

10 Things Every Student Needs to Know to Study **Video**
This 60-minute video covers such practical skills as note taking, test taking, and listening, among others. ISBN 1-4130-1533-6

10 Things Every Student Needs to Succeed in College **Video**
This 60-minute video compilation illustrates ten valuable and highly effective practices every student needs in order to engage in a successful college experience. Topics include successful time management, recognizing and understanding learning styles, and written/spoken communication. ISBN 1-4130-2907-8

Integrating Technology in the Classroom

Web Links

Time-Management Tips – http://www.gmu.edu/gmu/personal/time.html
George Mason University hosts this site, which gives instructions for taking a personal time survey as well as several useful ideas for better managing time.

Personal Goal Setting – http://www.time-management-guide.com/personal-goal-setting.html
This comprehensive site offers a wealth of information about personal goal setting, and how students can turn those goals into action plans.

Learn to Prioritize – http://www.suite101.com/article.cfm/17943/103703
Ask your students to read this article, which explains how learning to prioritize can reduce the level of stress in their lives, academic or otherwise.

Printable Checklists – http://www.allfreeprintables.com/checklists/to-do-lists.shtml
Direct your students to this site, where they can print out free "to do" lists. The site also offers free printable checklists for other activities such as grocery shopping and childproofing your home.

Procrastination Quiz – http://discoveryhealth.queendom.com/procrastination_short_access.html
This 15-minute online quiz identifies if your students are procrastinators, and if so, why and in which areas of their lives are most affected.

Wadsworth College Success –
http://www.wadsworth.com/colsuccess_d/special_features/studyskills/devsurskills/devsurskills_12.html
The Wadsworth College Success site offers some great tips for improving concentration. Encourage your students to try out one new method each week.

About Freshman Seminars

Today, the Freshman Year Experience movement in the U.S.A. is nearly three decades old and well integrated into American higher education (Barefoot & Fidler, 1996; Cuseo, 1991; Sax, Astin, Korn, William & Mahoney, 2001; Upcraft, Gardner & Barefoot, 2004). While this movement has sought to stitch success into all aspects of university life and has promoted many interventions to enhance student success, freshman seminars by themselves have successfully addressed many of the needs of freshman students and have "tackled a long standing, seemingly endemic problem for higher education, the confusion and difficulties that cause many new students to drop out of college during or at the end of their freshman year" (El-Khawas, 2002).

In the 1980s, as institutions of higher education became increasingly concerned about issues pointedly identified by Tinto (1975, 1987), such as, why do students leave and what factors contribute to student success, colleges and universities began to implement a variety of strategies to enhance freshman success and retention. To this end, many institutions sought to create and boost fledgling first-year seminars in an attempt to improve student involvement and increase student retention (Upcraft & Gardner, 1989).

The freshman seminar is a course designed to enhance the academic and/or social integration of first-year college students into the institution (Barefoot & Fidler, 1996; Gordon, 1989). In the 2000 National Survey of First-Year Seminar Programming conducted by the National Resource Center for the First-Year Experience and Students in Transition, five variations of freshman seminars were identified: *extended orientation* seminars, *academic* seminars with common content, *academic* seminars with variable content across sections, *basic study skills* seminars, and *professional* seminars. *Extended orientation* seminars were the most frequent type of freshman seminars reported and are more commonly referred to as "freshman orientation, college survival, or student success courses" (Linder, p. 1). The most frequently mentioned topics addressed in such seminars were: academic skills, time management, personal development and self-awareness, transition to college, and career exploration.

In their landmark work on the Freshman Year Experience, freshman success was defined by Upcraft and Gardner (1989) as making progress toward fulfilling educational and personal goals by: 1) developing academic and intellectual competence; 2) establishing and maintaining interpersonal relationships; 3) developing an identity; 4) deciding on a career and life-style; 5) maintaining personal health and wellness; and 6) developing an integrated philosophy of life. We find that nearly three decades later, freshman seminars continue to help students do that and more (Linder, 2002; Skipper, 2002). Of the responding institutions in the 2000 National Survey of First-Year Seminar Programming (*n* = 1,013), the majority of institutions had one or more of the following "research-based goals" for their freshman seminar:

- Enhancing academic skills
- Helping students transition to college and provide an orientation to campus resources
- Helping students improve their self-concept

The evidence is compelling that there is a positive correlation between participation in the freshman seminar and many desirable experiential outcomes for both students and faculty. Some of these outcomes include higher rates of freshman-to-sophomore retention, especially for minority students, higher graduation rates, higher grade point averages, more frequent out-of-class interaction with faculty, more involvement in campus organizations, more frequent use of helping services on campus, and greater faculty use of innovative teaching strategies—in the seminar and in other discipline-based classes

References

Barefoot, B. O., & Fidler, P. P. (1996). *The 1994 national survey of freshman seminar programs* (Monograph No. 20). Columbia, SC: University of South Carolina, National Resource Center for the First-Year Experience and Students in Transition.

Cuseo, J. B. (1991). *The freshman orientation seminar: A research-based rationale for its value, delivery, and content* (Monograph No. 4). Columbia, SC: University of South Carolina, National Resource Center for the First-Year Experience.

El-Khawas, E. (2002). Reform movements. In *Higher education in the United States: An encyclopedia* (Vol. 2, pp. 512-516). Santa Barbara, CA: ABC-CLIO, Inc.

Gordon, V. P. (1989). Origins and purpose of the freshman seminar. In M. L. Upcraft & J. N. Gardner (Eds.), *The Freshman Year Experience* (pp. 25-39). San Francisco: Jossey-Bass.

Linder, C. (2002). *The 2002 national survey of first-year seminar programs: Continuing innovations in the collegiate curriculum* (Monograph No. 35) (pp. 1-3). Columbia, SC: University of South Carolina.

Sax, L., Korn, A. W., & Mahoney, K. (2001) *The American freshman: National norms for Fall 2001,* 36th Annual Edition. Los Angeles: Higher Education Research Institute.

Tinto, V. (1975). Dropout from higher education: A theoretical synthesis of recent research. *Review of Educational Research, 45*, 89-125.

Tinto, V. (1987). *Leaving college: Rethinking the causes and cures of student attrition (2nd Ed.).* Chicago: University of Chicago Press.

Upcraft, M. L., Gardner, J. N., & Associates. (1989). *The freshman year experience.* San Francisco: Jossey-Bass.

Upcraft, M. L., Gardner, J. N., & B. O. Barefoot (2004). Meeting challenges and building support: Creating campus climates for first-year student success. San Francisco: Jossey-Bass.

Peer Leaders in the Freshman Seminar

Undoubtedly, this trend of using peer leaders in freshman seminars is growing and institutions are recognizing that students deliver a variety of services and assistance to their fellow students. In 1994, 8.2% of colleges and universities surveyed were using peer leaders in first-year seminars (National Resource Center for the First-Year Experience and Students in Transition). A recent survey by the Policy Center on the First-Year of College (2000), found that 25% were doing so. Why use peer leaders? The research clearly demonstrates that colleges and universities shape students' development and the impact of the peer group on individual students is powerful (Astin, 1993; Chickering, 1969; Heath, 1968). Research on peer teaching indicates that both the peer learner and the peer teacher learn significantly from collaborative learning experiences and that peer teachers demonstrate deeper levels of understanding for the information they convey to their peers and attain a stronger grasp for the course content (Bargh & Schul, 1980; Benware & Deci, 1984; Whitman, 1988).

Based on survey data from 31,661 students at 61 institutions, the National Study of First-Year Seminar Learning Outcomes conducted by the Policy Center on the First-Year of College (Swing, 2001) found that the use of undergraduate teaching assistants in freshman seminars was correlated with higher scores assigned to learning outcomes and satisfaction than those of students who participated in freshman seminars that did not use peer leaders. Gordon (1989) has emphasized that freshman seminars use pedagogical methods that facilitate active learning, high levels of interaction, and critical thinking. One of the ways by which these pedagogical methods are realized is through the peer support group, such as student groups and networks. Peers promote student-to-student interaction and the use of peer leaders to help facilitate first-year seminar courses (Gardner, 1996; Gardner & Hamid; 2001; Gardner & Hunter, 1999; Hamid & Vanhook, 2001). Such students are seen as "an invaluable resource to the first-year seminar when trained and empowered as part of a teaching team" (Strommer, 1999, p. 51).

The use of peer leaders in first-year seminars also appears to have a positive impact on the retention of first-year students. According to Tinto (1987), one of the major reasons for students dropping out of college is failure to establish a social network. Peer leaders are being used to bridge that gap. The positive effects of collaborative learning on student retention is documented in Tinto's (1987) research with adult students which revealed that the single most important predictor of students' persistence to graduation was whether they were members of a peer learning group. Freshman to sophomore retention rates at numerous institutions showed an increase in the rate of first-year to sophomore year retention by more than 6% (Hamid, 2001).

Following an extensive review of the literature on teaching and learning research in higher education, McKeachie (1986) concluded: "the best answer to the question of what is the most effective method of teaching is that it depends on the goal, the student, the content, and the teachers. But the next best answer is 'students teaching other students'" (p.63). In a similar vein, Gardner (1996) pronounced, "I have heard of freshman seminars literally coming and going from campuses… I have never heard of a freshman seminar that added the peer leader component and then subsequently dropped this feature of the course (p. 2).

Given the findings that peers exert influence on each other, it is no wonder that the use of outstanding student role models as peer leaders is one of the hottest trends in the freshman seminar course development in American higher education today (Gardner, 1996). Educators are recognizing and harnessing the tremendous potential value wrought by the use of students to facilitate learning and personal development. Indeed, it seems reasonable to conclude that students listen to their peers and learn a great deal, perhaps the most, from other students. Why not use peer leaders as co-teachers of your freshman seminar?

Special Note to Adjuncts
As an adjunct instructor, you face challenges that many full-time professors don't encounter—last minute course assignments, courses at multiple schools, and juggling your busy schedule without an office of your own.

With our Service Direct Website, you may browse our product catalog, and request and track review or desk copies for your classes 24-hours a day, seven days a week, right from your desktop!

Please visit http://servicedirect.thomsonlearning.com/servicedirect/adjunct/default.aspx to register now and see how Service Direct can work for you.

References

Astin, A. W., (1993). *What matters in college? Four critical years revisited.* San Francisco: Jossey-Bass.

Bargh, J. A., & Schul, Y. (1980). On the cognitive benefits of teaching. *Journal of Educational Psychology, 72,* 593-604.

Benware, C. A., & Deci, E. L. (1984). Quality of learning with an active versus passive motivational set. *American Educational Research Journal, 21,* 755-765.

Chickering, A. W., (1969). *Education and identity.* San Francisco: Jossey-Bass.

Gardner, J. N., & Hamid, S. L. (2001). *Summary and recommendations.* In S. L. Hamid (Ed.), *Peer Leadership: A primer on program essentials* (Monograph No 32) (pp. 97-102). Columbia, SC: University of South Carolina, National Resource Center for the First-Year Experience and Students in Transition.

Gardner, J. N., & Hunter, M. S. (1999). *Outcomes and future directions of instructor training programs.* (Monograph No. 29) (pp. 107-110). Columbia, SC: University of South Carolina, National Resource Center for the First-Year Experience and Students in Transition.

Gardner, J. N., (1996). "Power to Peers." *Keystone Newsletter.* Belmont, CA. Wadsworth Publishing Company.

Gordon, V. P. (1989). Origins and purpose of the freshman seminar. In M. L. Upcraft & J. N. Gardner (Eds.), *The Freshman Year Experience* (pp. 25-39). San Francisco: Jossey-Bass.

Hamid, S. L., & VanHook, J., (2001). *First-year seminar peer leaders, programs and profiles.* (Monograph No 32). Columbia, SC: University of South Carolina, National Resource Center for the First-Year Experience and Students in Transition.

Heath, D. H. (1968). *Growing up in college.* San Francisco: Jossey-Bass.

McKeachie, W. J. (1986). *Teaching tips*, (8th ed.) Lexington, MA: D.C. Heath.

Strommer, D. W. (1999). *Teaching college students: Ten tips for success.* (Monograph No. 29) (pp. 107-110). Columbia, SC: University of South Carolina, National Resource Center for the First-Year Experience and Students in Transition.

Swing, R. (2001). *First national study of first-year seminar learning outcomes,* 2001. Unpublished summary. Available: Policy Center on the First-Year of College, Brevard College, Brevard, NC.

Tinto, V. (1987). *Leaving college: Rethinking the causes and cures of student attrition (2nd Ed.).* Chicago: University of Chicago Press.

Whitman, C.E. & Underwood, V.L. (1985). Learning strategies: The how of learning. In J.W. Segal, S.F. Chapman, and R. Glasser (Eds.), *Thinking and Learning Skills* (pp. 241-258). Hillsdale, NJ: Lawrence Erlbaum.

The College Success Factors Index: An Instructor's How-To Guide

Developed by Gary J. Williams, Ed.D. Long Beach City College,
Long Beach, CA

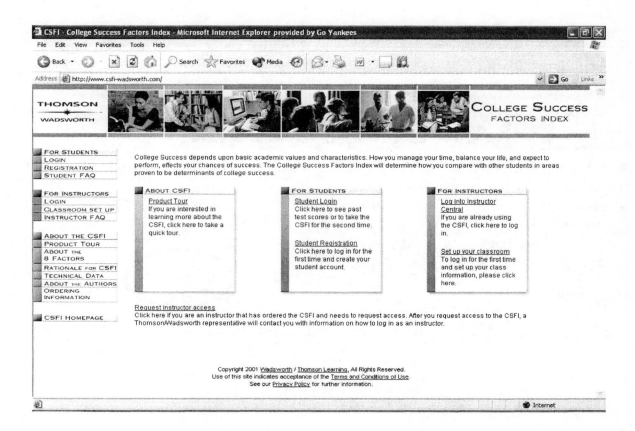

This guide is designed to be a simple how-to guide on how to get started using the College Success Factors Index (also known as the CSFI). In this guide, you will receive step-by-step instructions on:

- How to register your own instructor account on the CSFI website.
- How to set up your class on the CSFI website.
- What your students need to know and do in order to complete the CSFI on the Internet.
- How to access the CSFI results for your class, and what your next steps should be.
- Developing intervention strategies for your class using the CSFI, including a few brief examples.
- What to do if you or your students lose their access codes or passwords.
- How to contact Thomson Wadsworth's College Success Division if you have questions or need assistance.

I. Getting Started: Setting up your classroom on the CSFI Website:

Getting started using the College Success Factors Index is easy. Simply visit http://success.wadsworth.com/gardner7e and follow the link to the CSFI website.

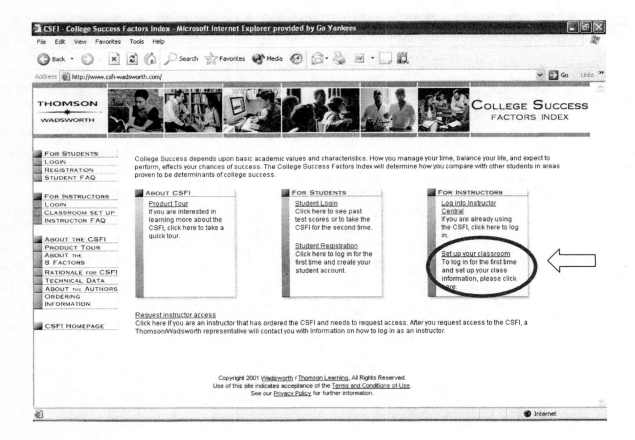

Your first task is to set up your own personal instructor account. To do so, follow these steps:

1. Click "Set up your classroom" link as indicated in the illustration above.
2. You will then be asked for a "School Password" as shown below. You can request a school password by e-mail at csuccess@thomson.com.

3. Next, you will be asked to provide the following registration information:

Be sure to write down your login name and password, as you will use this to access the CSFI website from this point on.

4. Should you forget your login or password, you can request them by e-mail at csuccess@thomson.com.

II. Instructor Central

Now that you have registered as an instructor, all the resources you need are located in one place on the CSFI website. Instructor Central is where you will go to set up your classes, to take the CSFI, access student results, and to find information about each of the 8 Factors, as well as strategies to address student needs.

To access Instructor Central, you must first log in by using the login name and password you just created. Navigate your browser to the CSFI website and click "Log into Instructor Central" as shown at the top of the next page.

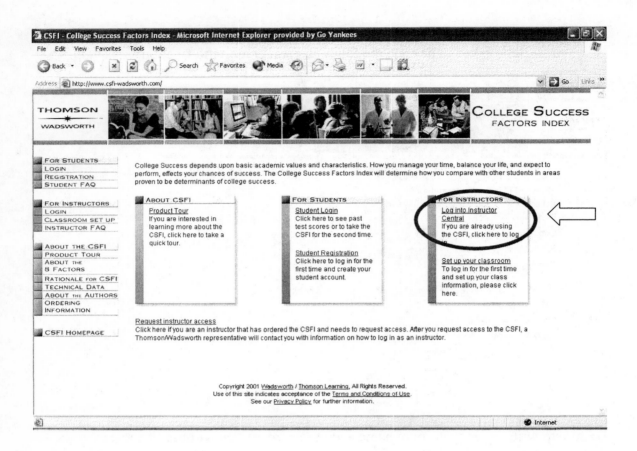

Next, provide your User Name and Password:

LOG IN TO INSTRUCTOR CENTRAL
Enter your username and password.

User Name _____

Password _____

[Login]

Before you can log in, you must register and set up a new classroom. To register
and set up a new classroom, please click here.

You are then taken to the "Instructor Central" page, which is shown below:

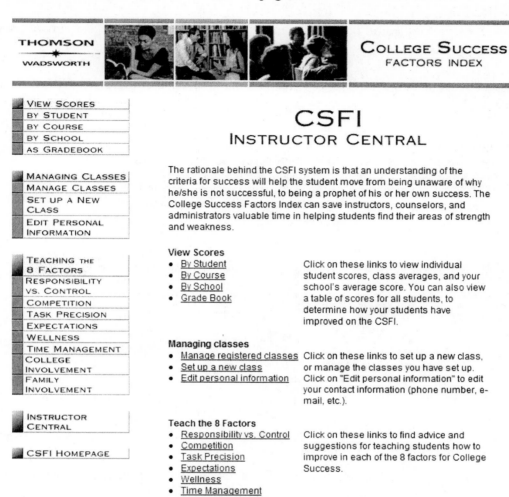

THOMSON
WADSWORTH

COLLEGE SUCCESS
FACTORS INDEX

VIEW SCORES
BY STUDENT
BY COURSE
BY SCHOOL
AS GRADEBOOK

MANAGING CLASSES
MANAGE CLASSES
SET UP A NEW
CLASS
EDIT PERSONAL
INFORMATION

TEACHING THE
8 FACTORS
RESPONSIBILITY
VS. CONTROL
COMPETITION
TASK PRECISION
EXPECTATIONS
WELLNESS
TIME MANAGEMENT
COLLEGE
INVOLVEMENT
FAMILY
INVOLVEMENT

INSTRUCTOR
CENTRAL

CSFI HOMEPAGE

CSFI
INSTRUCTOR CENTRAL

The rationale behind the CSFI system is that an understanding of the criteria for success will help the student move from being unaware of why he/she is not successful, to being a prophet of his or her own success. The College Success Factors Index can save instructors, counselors, and administrators valuable time in helping students find their areas of strength and weakness.

View Scores
- By Student
- By Course
- By School
- Grade Book

Click on these links to view individual student scores, class averages, and your school's average score. You can also view a table of scores for all students, to determine how your students have improved on the CSFI.

Managing classes
- Manage registered classes
- Set up a new class
- Edit personal information

Click on these links to set up a new class, or manage the classes you have set up. Click on "Edit personal information" to edit your contact information (phone number, e-mail, etc.).

Teach the 8 Factors
- Responsibility vs. Control
- Competition
- Task Precision
- Expectations
- Wellness
- Time Management
- College Involvement
- Family Involvement

Click on these links to find advice and suggestions for teaching students how to improve in each of the 8 factors for College Success.

From this page, you can view student and class scores and results, set up new classes and manage existing classes, and read all about strategies you can use to help your students get the most from their experience using the CSFI.

In the following section, we will cover how you can set up your class to take the CSFI.

III. Setting up a new class to take the CSFI

From the Instructor Central page, you can easily set up your class (or as many classes as you wish) to take the CSFI.

1. Click on "Set up a new class" link, which is located under the Managing Classes heading, as indicated below:

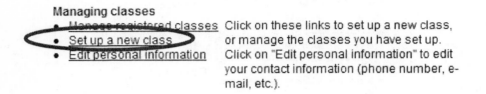

2. You will then be taken to the "Set up a new class" registration screen:

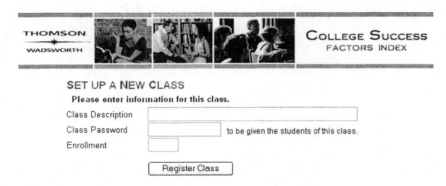

3. Provide a brief description of the class you are registering, and the number of students in that class under the enrollment screen. If you wish to register several classes, register each of them separately, using a separate description for each class.

4. **The Class Password is very important**. You will be providing this password to your students in each class section you set up and the students will need it when they register to take the CSFI. Make sure it is not a personal password that you do not wish to disclose to others. Also, you will need a different password for each class you set up. It helps to make them easy-to-remember for the students. Provide this password to them in writing, such as on a note card or in the syllabus.

   The class password is also important because it is what uniquely identifies your student in the CSFI website database as part of the class you set up. If students were to use a different class password than the one you establish for your class, their results would not appear when you attempt to access student scores from the Instructor Central page. It is vital that you ensure that students use only the class password that you give them.

5. Once you've clicked on "Register Class," you are ready to have your students take the CSFI.

IV. Administering the CSFI to your students

Because the CSFI is a web-based assessment, students can access the instrument in a number of settings - in a computer lab, at home, or wherever they can access the Internet. As an instructor, you have the flexibility of choosing to assign the CSFI as an out-of-class activity, or have students take the instrument all at once in a computer lab setting. Whether students take it individually or together as a class, the steps to completing the CSFI are the same.

1. Students will navigate their browser to the CSFI website: http://www.csfi-wadsworth.com and click on "Student Registration" as shown below:

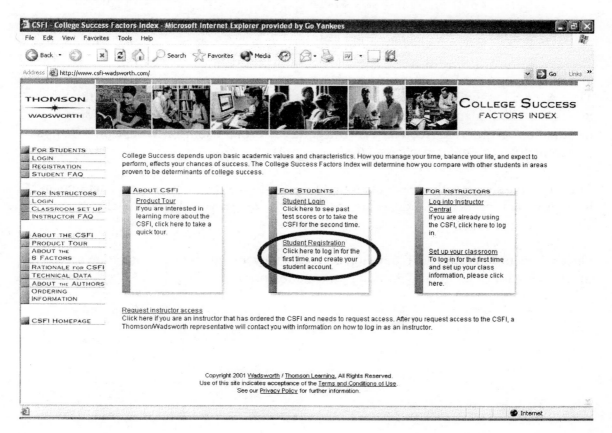

2. Students are required to enter two passwords to access the CSFI on the web:

STUDENT REGISTRATION
Please your access password and your class password

Your **access password** can be found on the back of the card that came with your textbook. Enter your access password in the text box below.

[   ]

Your professor should have given you a unique **class password** to enter the CSFI. Enter your class password in the text box below.

[   ]

If you do not have your class password, please see your instructor.

[Enter]

The "Access Password" is provided on a card provided by Thomson Wadsworth, either bundled in the student textbook or sold separately by Thomson Wadsworth. (For information on ordering Access Password cards, see your Thomson Wadsworth Campus representative, or e-mail csuccess@thomson.com)

The Class Password is the one that you established for the class in the previous step and have provided for them. Students are instructed to contact you should they lose their Class Password.

3. Once students enter the two required passwords, they are taken to a registration screen to input their name and other identifying information prior to taking the CSFI:

STUDENT REGISTRATION

You Are Approved for taking "Student Success/Transfer Services Center "

Please fill out this form and submit it for our records

First Name [ ]

Last Name [ ]

Gender Male ○
Female ○

Birth Date [ ] / [ ] / [ ] (mm/dd/yyyy)

Ethnic Background [African American (not of Hispanic origin) ▼]

Other Ethnic Background [ ]

What was your high school Grade Point Average (GPA)?
[A to A- (4.0 - 3.5) ▼]

How many college credits have you completed?
[None ▼]

What is your college Grade Point Average (GPA)? (If this is your first semester in college, select "First semester.")
[A to A- (4.0 - 3.5) ▼]

Who asked you to take the CSFI?
[Course Instructor ▼]

What is your degree goal?
[Associates ▼]

Remember to write down your login and password for future use.

Please Choose a login name [ ]

Choose a Password [ ]

Verify your Password [ ]

[Enter]

Students are asked to choose a login name and password, which will serve as their access to the CSFI website from this point forward. In other words, the access and class passwords are no longer required once the student has completed the student registration form. Emphasize to students that they must write down their login name and password.

4. Once students have successfully registered, they are given access to the CSFI assessment.

CSFI
STUDENT CENTRAL

Take the CSFI assessment
If you are ready to begin the 80-question assessment,
click on the link above.

5. To begin the assessment, they click on the link to "Take the CSFI assessment," and after reading the test instructions, they can begin the assessment.

6. The assessment consists of 80 items, where students are asked to indicate their response by clicking on the bubble that most closely matches their view of each statement as it pertains to their attitudes and practices as a student.

CSFI ASSESSMENT		Strongly Agree	Agree	Undecided	Disagree	Strongly Disagree
#	Statement					Page 1 of 10
1.	I involve myself with a lot of school or college projects.	O	O	O	O	O
2.	People should stand up for what they believe.	O	O	O	O	O
3.	I can handle examination stress.	O	O	O	O	O
4.	Competition at college is necessary for success.	O	O	O	O	O
5.	I know why my career choice requires a college degree.	O	O	O	O	O
6.	I am a strong competitor when I need to be.	O	O	O	O	O
7.	My family will definitely attend my graduation.	O	O	O	O	O
8.	My life rarely gets out of hand.	O	O	O	O	O
#	Statement	Strongly Agree	Agree	Undecided	Disagree	Strongly Disagree

Next →

24

7. Once students have answered item 80, they will click on the button titled "Score Test" and their results will be displayed on screen as shown below:

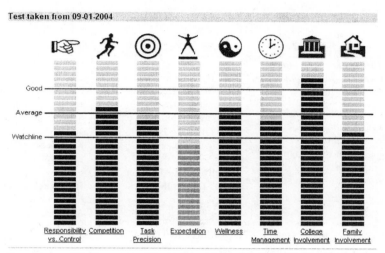

Test taken from 09-01-2004

The graph above shows how you stand in each of the eight factors that constitute the College Success Factors Index (or CSFI). The CSFI is not a test you pass or fail, but it does represent a set of characteristics critical to college success.

Look at the red areas where your score falls below the watchline. These are the areas that need improvement first.

At the same moment, the students' results are stored in the CSFI website database under the class associated with the class password that you provided. Simultaneously, an e-mail is generated to your e-mail account (the one you provided when you registered as an instructor), indicating the name of the student who just completed the CSFI assessment. You are now able to view the students' scores by logging into Instructor Central using your own login and password.

Toll-Free Academic Resource Center for CSFI
Please call (800) 423-0563 if you have any questions or concerns regarding the College Success Factors Index.

Chapter 1: Strategies for Success

Ideas for Instruction and Instructor Training	Video and CD-ROMs	Media Resources for Instructors	Media Resources for Students
Instructor's Manual (IM) Includes a brief lesson plan for Chapter 1, chapter objectives, lecture launchers, commentary on exercises in the book, and case studies. **Test Bank (in IM)** Multiple Choice, True/False, Short Answer and Essay Questions. Also available in ExamView® electronic format, which can be customized to fit your needs.	*10 Things Every Student Needs to Succeed in College* **Video** 60-minute video covers valuable practices, such as successful time management, recognizing and understanding learning styles, and written/spoken communication. *10 Things Every Student Needs to Know to Study* **Video** 60-minute video covers practical skills, such as note taking, test taking, and listening. **ExamView® CD-ROM** Computerized version of the Test Bank items for Chapter 1.	JOININ™ Hand-held audience response device allows students immediate response to multiple-choice questions, polls, and interactive exercises. **Multimedia Manager 2007 CD-ROM** PowerPoint preentations, video clips, images, and web links help with assembly, editing, and presentation of multimedia lectures.	**iLrn® Pin-Coded Website** Contains self-assessments, electronic journals that encourage students to reflect on their progress, essay questions and exercises, and Test Your Knowledge interactive quizzes for chapter 1. **InfoTrac® College Edition** May be bundled with text. *Keywords:* college success, liberal arts, goal setting, values, colleges, universities. **WebTutor™ Toolbox** Online course management tool for WebCT™ or Blackboard preloaded with text-specific content and media resources for Chapter 1.

A. Chapter Objectives

1. To introduce factors which contribute to college success
2. To illustrate some of the challenges students will face as they begin their college education
3. To secure students' understanding of the outcomes of a college education
4. To establish a process of setting goals and encourage students to set goals that will contribute to their persistence

B. Timing of Chapter Coverage

This chapter should be assigned and discussed at the beginning of the course. It is essentially an overview of both the text and the course itself. It sets up the basic strategies which will be used throughout the book, including planning ahead, taking charge of your learning, developing good learning skills, getting connected, and knowing yourself.

C. About This Chapter

Beginning college students often hold contradictory beliefs about their new environment. On the one hand, they believe they have been successful thus far in their lives and will continue to be successful. On the other hand, they've heard from older siblings and friends who have been to college that college is significantly different from high school. Thus, they're really not quite sure that what worked in high school and in the world of work and the home will also work in college. As one student put it, "There's a kind of magic that some students have and others don't, and I hope I can discover the secret myself!"

The purpose of this chapter is to introduce your students to the secret, which is anything *but* magic. Rather, the secret to college success is to establish a deliberate, rational plan to guide their academic and extracurricular life. In presenting strategies, the authors of the textbook base their recommendations on an understanding of the research about retention/persistence (in particular, the research of Alexander Astin, Vincent Tinto, and E.T. Pascarella). This research shows correlations between specific student behaviors and persistence through graduation. Although these are simply correlations (and not causal relationships), they do suggest ways to help students adopt positive behaviors that will increase their chances of completing a degree. The following topics in this chapter book are intended to show students that they can beat these odds.

The section on **Strategies for Success** constitutes a touchstone that you can use throughout the course to test students' plans of action. Take time at the beginning of the course to present these strategies as simple, positive steps to success. Addressing these strategies (plan ahead, take charge of learning, sharpen your skills, get connected, and know yourself) will offer students some positive ways to increase their chances of completing a degree. Many of the persistence factors are revisited later on in the book. Students need to recognize early that it is important that they make adjustments and establish a deliberate, rational plan to guide their academic and extracurricular life. Addressing the topic of **high school versus college** is one way to do this; it will emphasize to the students the major differences between high school and college and offer suggestions to help them make the adjustments to college life. When you present this material on high school versus college, encourage students to use the chapter as a guide to understanding the changes they should expect in their first year and to think more deeply about these issues; finally, at the end of the term, you can return to the discussion and ask students to reflect on how they actually have changed.

The primary reason most students attend college is to prepare themselves for careers that will increase their economic security throughout their lives. The chapter goes on to explore some of the other reasons. However, while it is important to make the students aware of the value of a college education, traditional-aged students may not fully understand the significance of these abstractions this early in their college career. Of course, they'll understand the words, but will the words have the necessary impact? Try to use the nontraditional students as examples to help make the abstractions concrete.

Students need to be reminded, even informed, of the "help" that is readily available to them on campus and that by utilizing these services, their success as students could be insured. The section on page 14, **Where to Go for Help on Campus,** is crucial information for new students and they should be reminded about the importance of finding help and utilizing campus resources.

One of the basic threads of *Your College Experience, Seventh Edition*, is the importance of **goal setting**. In fact, student success is linked to this process from the book's beginning to its end. Students who establish a deliberate plan of action for themselves significantly increase their chances for success. Thus, it is important at the beginning of the term to take up goal setting, and the exercises in Chapter 1 are a good starting point. Because this is the beginning of the term and your class is not yet built into a group, the personal nature of the exercises may preclude an open discussion about personal goals. It is important, however, that the exercises be processed.

D. Suggested Outline for Addressing Topics in Chapter 1

STEP I: BEGIN WITH A LECTURE LAUNCHER OR ICEBREAKER ACTIVITY
STEP II: EMPLOY A VARIETY OF CLASSROOM ACTIVITIES
    a. Use the PowerPoint presentation from *Multimedia Manager 2007* resource
    b. Expand on key lesson themes
    c. Involve peer leaders
    d. Make use of chapter exercises
    e. Engage students in learning through case studies
STEP III: REVIEW & PREVIEW
    a. Address common questions and concerns about the topic
    b. Writing reflection
    c. Prepare for next class

Expanded Lesson Plan

STEP I: Lecture Launchers and Icebreakers

- Since this is the first chapter/week of the term, a good introduction is to have students participate in a variation of the **Name Game**. In this exercise, students introduce themselves by adding an adjective in front of their name that begins with the same letter or sound ("I'm Awesome Amy," "I'm Cool Kristina"). The trick is that each subsequent student must begin by listing all of the other students who were introduced before (similar to the game: I'm Going On a Picnic). The instructor should be the first and last to participate. This aids in name recognition both for the students and the instructor.

- A second icebreaker that's helpful is to have students interview each other. One way to approach this is to have students line up across the back of the room by their birthdays, with January on one end and December on the other. Then ask them to pair with someone next to them (this almost always assures they will pair up with a stranger). Have them interview one another (name, hometown, major, future goals, etc.). Give them five minutes and then ask students to introduce their partner to the rest of the class.

- Generate a class discussion about some of the changes students have had to make in order to adapt to university life.

- Plan a dialogue between you and a former student (or your peer leader) and discuss the background, qualities, and expectations of a good teacher and a good student

STEP II: Classroom Activities

a. Use the PowerPoint presentation in *Multimedia Manager 2007* to complement your mini lecture.

b. Key Lesson Themes

- Discuss the purpose for taking this course. Explain the **syllabus** and answer any questions students may have. The more your students understand the syllabus, the better they will understand the course. Introduce the required assignments and expectations for the semester. Introduce the course calendar, highlighting **due dates**. Make sure that the students understand *how* to read the course **calendar** if you have one. Highlight the components of each chapter in the book. This will help the students become familiar with the text and make it a user-friendly book.

- Emphasize the *Strategies for Success* on pp. 5-8.

- If your class is willing to open up, this might be a good time to have a **question and answer session** regarding their concerns. Many students are probably beginning to have hundreds of questions and fears about life in college. You might have better luck if you invite the students to write their questions, fears, or concerns on an index card. Make sure you let them know that they are not required to identify themselves. Collect all of the cards and answer accordingly. You could refer to **Exercise 1.3.**

c. Group Activities

- Generate a class discussion about your school's heritage and highlight some of the positive rituals and traditions of your university. Introduce students to a community creed or covenant if you have one; if not, provide an example of one. Ask students to get into small groups and create a creed. You can also blend in discussion of negative self-talk and how to avoid it.

- Divide the class into groups of four or five (depending on class size). Then ask the groups to each do the following:

  1. Construct an argument intended to convince the class of the need for studying this success factor.
  2. Present the argument to the class as a whole.

- These presentations will provide the basis for group discussion and allow you to stress the importance of these factors. At the end of the session, ask the class to vote on which factors are most important to cover early in the course, later in the course, and so forth. Because you are using this exercise to build the group into a coherent, working unit and to highlight the importance of these persistence factors, do not grade these presentations. The sooner your students begin to apply these factors to their behavior, the greater their chances of success. Throughout the term, you should continue to stress the importance of these success factors.

- Another option is to create permanent peer groups within the course. Assign students to different "teams," either randomly or with certain criteria in mind (i.e., consider factors such as gender or major to help divide the students into a diverse mix). Give the students time to get to know one another, either over an activity (such as the one listed above) or perhaps the interviewing icebreaker suggested earlier. Before you end the session, have each group choose a name for their team.

d. Peer Leader Assistance

- Distribute **index cards**. Ask your students to share some information about themselves: telephone number, e-mail address, birthday, campus box number, etc (if they choose to do so). Compile a list with the names, numbers, and addresses of the students and give a copy to each student. Do not forget to include your numbers. Use the e-mail addresses to create a **list-serve** and the numbers to give your students a **phone call** during their first week of college.

- Give a **testimonial** endorsing the "Strategies for Success," how and why you succeeded in the college setting, or why you chose to attend college/university.

- Give a testimonial on your academic career at your university. Be sure to include the qualities/ingredients that helped to make you a successful student. Share with the class some of the changes you have had to make to adapt to university life. Describe the faculty at your university whom you considered to be your mentor. Conclude with the role that person has played in your success as a student and as an individual.

- As a follow-up to this initial session, consider giving each of your students a call during their first week of college. Find out if they have any questions about the course, the syllabus, or the text. (This would be a good time to use that "extra" information you requested on the index cards.)

e. Case Studies

Alicia
Alicia is going to school and working a full-time job. Her employer generally supports her decision to be in college, but Alicia thinks her boss is asking her to take on more

responsibilities than her schedule allows. Alicia decides to arrange a meeting in which she hopes they can both talk frankly about the problem, but she worries that her boss will think she's being "a complainer."

Discussion Questions:
1. What should Alicia do to prepare for her meeting with her boss?
2. List some possible ways that Alicia's boss might respond to the issues she plans to raise in their meeting. For example, her boss might be angry or resentful that Alicia is asking to have some of her responsibilities reassigned. How can Alicia "plead her case" without sounding like the "complainer" she fears she will be perceived as?
3. If Alicia's boss refuses to reduce her workload, what should Alicia do?

Sarah
It's Friday and Sarah just got a weekend extension on the history essay that was due today. Friday evening her boyfriend calls and says he wants to drive up and spend the weekend with her. She knows why he wants to come: It's because he's still nervous about their being in different cities. She doesn't think she can afford to socialize all weekend. She wonders if he understands how worried she is about her courses.

Discussion Questions:
1. Should Sarah agree to the impromptu visit with her boyfriend?
2. What factors do you think led to Sarah's need for an extension in the first place?
3. How might Sarah better manage her time so that she can complete her assignments by the due date *and* still spend time with her boyfriend?

Carlos
Carlos thinks his mother has some unrealistic expectations. She likes to tell him that the reason she never finished college was so she could work and give her children the chance to go. Now she expects Carlos to come through his first year with A's in all his courses. Carlos doesn't do all that well on his initial round of exams, and when his mother hears the results, she expresses her disappointment and lectures him about whether or not he's serious about the education she's paying for.

Discussion Questions:
1. What are some possible reasons for Carlos's lackluster performance?
2. How do you think Carlos responded to his mother's lecture? How would you have responded?
3. What are some strategies for success that Carlos can employ to help improve his grades on future exams?

f. Chapter Exercises

*   **Exercise 1.1: Solving a Problem**

This is one of those exercises that should not be graded, and you should tell your student this before they complete it.

- **Exercise 1.2: With or Without**
  You might have students complete this exercise at the beginning of a class session. Consider placing them in small groups to discuss the lists they've generated. This will not only prompt discussion, but it will facilitate group bonding.

STEP III: Review and Preview

REVIEW

a. Address Common Questions and Concerns of First-Year Students:

- *Why do I have to worry about setting goals? I like to go with the flow.*
  Answer: Setting goals is the first step toward achievement. It helps students to combat negative self-fulfilling prophecies and allows them to form positive ones.

- *Commitment issues? I had no trouble getting through high school!*
  Answer: Forty percent of all students who enroll in four-year schools never finish their degrees, but by applying certain learned strategies, students can set themselves up for success.

- *As a commuter, can I live at home and still be successful?*
  Answer: Commuter students should try to maximize their commuting time, either by reviewing notes (if taking public transportation), discussing issues (if commuting with a classmate), or even listening to taped lectures or notes they've recorded (especially useful for long car rides).

- *After being out of school for so many years, can I make it?*
  Answer: Of course you can make it. Sometimes returning students are the most diligent ones in the class. Of course they face special challenges.

- *Why do "they" want to change me? I like the way I am!*
  Answer: College will naturally change a person. Benefits of college include a lower divorce rate, a better appreciation of the arts, and greater self-esteem.

- *Why are "they" asking me to take courses that raise issues about politics and other cultures? I just want to take courses that relate to my major and career.*
  Answer: Stress to your students the importance of a liberal arts education, and how courses that initially may not seem applicable to their major and career can be highly beneficial in the long run.

b. Writing Reflection

- At the start or at the end of class, assign your students a ten-minute free write. Let them know even before you give them the topic that this assignment will not be graded. Then pose a writing prompt – perhaps one of the journal topics suggested in the text. Another idea is to ask your students to write about which strategy for success they think will be the easiest for them to master, as well as which will be the hardest. This not only gives you a taste of their writing ability, it also lets you know where their perceived weaknesses lie. If several students express concern about the same strategy, you will then know to focus extra attention on that strategy. After the writing exercise, ask your students if any of them care to share what they've written. You can then use this to either help generate a class discussion, or as a good summary to the session.

- If you require your students to write a journal, ask them to include the exercises in the week's journal so that you can comment on them.

- You could require your students to submit the exercises as an out-of-class assignment, which you should then comment on and return as soon as possible.

- Set up individual appointments to discuss the goals and strategies. Obviously, this is a time-consuming suggestion, but conferencing is one of the most effective ways to reach a student. It is particularly appropriate if you are your students' advisor.

- Ask students to turn in completed exercises and use them as a way to gauge the attitudes and feelings of the group. Post the comments, but not the names of the students who made them. Exercise judgment: If a particularly sensitive situation is mentioned, leave it out and contact the student for a private appointment.

PREVIEW FOR NEXT CLASS

Ask students to complete Exercise 2.3. Have them record how they spend their time over a week or, if that seems too daunting, then over a handful of days. Ask them to bring the results to the next class. Ask students to bring all of their class syllabi to the next class.

E. Test Questions

Multiple Choice - choose ONE answer per question.

1. The most dangerous classes to miss are
   a. at the start of the term.
   b. the third week of the semester.
   c. before an exam.
   d. all of the above

2. If you are a full-time student, it is recommended that you limit your work week to

a. 20 hours.
b. 30 hours.
c. 25 hours.
d. 15 hours.

3. Research has found that students who involve themselves in class discussions
   a. don't take comprehensive notes.
   b. are teased by their peers.
   c. earn higher grades.
   d. don't remember much of what is discussed.

4. Today, more than _____ of high school graduates go on to college.
   a. 30%
   b. 55%
   c. 60%
   d. 75%

5. Research shows that studying with a group
   a. results in students completing less work than if they were studying on their own.
   b. provides a good distraction for students who are easily bored.
   c. helps students earn better grades and avoid more academic problems.
   d. doesn't help nor hurt a student's chance of success.

6. The highest college dropout rate occurs in the _____ year of college.
   a. first
   b. second
   c. third
   d. fourth

7. According to the text, if you are perpetually late with assignments you run the risk of
   a. receiving a grade penalty.
   b. irritating your teacher.
   c. a and b
   d. none of the above

8. If you need a job, whenever possible, look for one
   a. off campus.
   b. on campus.
   c. closer to your home.
   d. none of the above

9. Stress is the enemy of learning. If stressed,
   a. stay busy.
   b. enroll part-time.

    c. concentrate on one subject.

    d. none of the above

10. Plagiarism is a cause for severe disciplinary action, such as _____.

True/False

11. Research shows that independent study leads to higher grades than studying in groups.

12. Employers are looking for employees who can *think* and *write* and *speak*.

13. A college education will help you save money and make better investments.

14. It doesn't matter if your family is supportive of your education.

15. You should try to meet with your instructors one-on-one.

Short Answer

16. List the five key strategies for succeeding in college identified by your text.

17. Name two ways you can "sharpen your skills."

18. Give one example of a short-term goal and one of a long-term goal.

19. List two great investments you can make to help you manage your time.

20. List three ways to develop your critical thinking skills.

Essay

21. Relate the five key strategies for succeeding in college to some other area of your life, such as a hobby or extracurricular activity you've been involved in.

22. Identify and describe the strengths you possess which will be an asset to your completing your college education. Consider what might contribute to your risk of not finishing college, and how you think you can best address potential obstacles.

23. Describe a plan of action on how you plan to improve your writing and speaking over the coming semester.

24. Identify one staff or faculty person who cares about you and conduct an interview with that person.

25. Find out all you can about a specific club or organization you are interested in joining and write an essay explaining how and why becoming a member of this club can help you as a student.

Chapter 1 Answer Key

1. a, p. 5
2. d, p. 5
3. c, p. 6
4. c, p.12
5. b, p. 7
6. a, p. 4
7. c, p. 5
8. b, p. 6
9. b, p. 6
10. dismissal from school
11. false, p. 6
12. false, p. 7
13. true, p. 6
14. true, p. 12
15. false, p. 13
16. true, p. 13
17. Plan ahead, take charge of learning, hone your skills, get connected, know yourself, pp. 6-9
18. Any of the following: participate in class, learn how to remember more from every class, learn from criticism, take workshops on how to study, learn how to use the library and computer resources to conduct research.
19. Answers will vary.
20. A portable appointment calendar, a computer calendar program, or PDA, p.5

F. Web Resources

Benefits of a College Education – http://www.ihep.com/Org.php?parm=Press/PR6.htm
You may direct your students to this 1998 press release, issued by the Institute for Higher Education Policy, announcing a report that "indicates that the benefits of a college education are more extensive and significant than generally recognized." There is a hyperlink to a PDF file of the actual report as well.

About Goal Setting – http://www.about-goal-setting.com/
This online tutorial takes roughly 20 minutes to complete; it showcases the "science of goal-setting" and how to apply it to your life.

Study Distraction Analysis - www.ucc.vt.edu/stdysk/studydis.html

Tips for International Students - www.dartmouth.edu/admin/acskills/intl.html

Goal-Setting for Academic Success - www.siue.edu/SPIN/activity.html, nz.com/webnz/checkers/stdskll2.html

G. For More Information

Bronson, Po. (2002). *What should I do with my life? The true story of people who answered the ultimate question.* New York: Random House.

Chopra, Deepak. (1994). *The seven spiritual laws of success: A practical guide to the fulfillment of your dreams.* San Rafael, CA: Publishers Group West.

Combs, Patrick and Jack Canfield. (2003). *Major in success: Make college easier, fire up your dreams, and get a very cool job (4th ed).* Berkeley, CA: Ten Speed Press.

Covey, Stephen R. (1989). *The seven habits of highly effective people: Restoring the character ethic.* New York: Simon and Schuster.

Staley, Constance C. (1998). *Teaching college success: The complete resource guide.* Belmont, CA: Wadsworth.

Chapter 2: Time Management

By Jeanne L. Higbee, Professor and Faculty Chair, Center for Research on Developmental Education and Urban Literacy, General College, University of Minnesota

Ideas for Instruction and Instructor Training	Videos and CD-ROMs	Media Resources for Instructors	Media Resources for Students
Instructor's Manual (IM) Includes a brief lesson plan for Chapter 2, chapter objectives, lecture launchers, commentary on exercises in the book, and case studies. **Test Bank (in IM)** Multiple Choice, True/False, Short Answer and Essay Questions. Also available in ExamView® electronic format, which can be customized to fit your needs.	***10 Things Every Student Needs to Succeed in College* Video** 6-minute segment entitled "Successful Time Management." ***10 Things Every Student Needs to Know to Study* Video** 6-minute segment entitled "Managing Your Time." **ExamView® CD-ROM** Computerized version of the Test Bank items for Chapter 2.	**JOININ™** Hand-held audience response device allows students immediate response to multiple-choice questions, polls, and interactive exercises. **Multimedia Manager 2007 CD-ROM** PowerPoint presentations, video clips, images, and web links help with assembly, editing, and presentation of multimedia lectures.	**iLrn® Pin-Coded Website** Contains self-assessments, electronic journals that encourage students to reflect on their progress, essay questions and exercises, and Test Your Knowledge interactive quizzes for chapter 2. **InfoTrac® College Edition** May be bundled with text. *Keywords:* college success, liberal arts, goal setting, values, colleges, universities. **WebTutor™ Toolbox** Online course management tool for WebCT™ or Blackboard preloaded with text-specific content and media resources for Chapter 2.

A. Chapter Objectives

1. To demonstrate that time management is one of the strategies to success in college and in life
2. To explain how using goals and objectives can guide planning
3. To establish the importance of setting priorities
4. To demonstrate how students can use a daily planner and other tools
5. To illustrate how students can avoid distractions and combat procrastination

B. Timing of Chapter Coverage

It is critical that students actively engage in organizing their time from the outset of the academic term. Although some students may not appreciate the importance of developing skills in time management—at least until they experience a sense of losing control over their time—it is important to link early information about time management to some of the differences between high school and college. For students who tend to ignore time management techniques, assigning tasks that require them to plan will assist them in the long run. Procrastinators will get a better idea of why they behave as they do when they explore learning styles and personality types later in the text.

C. About This Chapter

Students often do not want to "waste" time on planning and managing their time. They may think that these activities take more time than they are worth. They may also resist exercises that they perceive to be "busy work." One way to motivate students and to involve them in the activities in this chapter is to focus on time management as a life skill rather than as a study skill. For those who did not get into the habit of maintaining a planner in high school, and do not necessarily intend to do so now, discuss how professionals use these tools in the world of work. Focus on how organizing one's time can assist in reducing stress. Today's students find more usefulness in maintaining a planner than in filling out a schedule form.

Whereas good time managers usually know they are good at managing their time, poor time managers may not be aware of how and when they waste time. This is especially true for students who were able to survive in high school without devoting a lot of time to schoolwork, or without developing organizational strategies. Asking students to assess their attitudes toward time before they actually begin to keep a record of how they spend their time sensitizes them to their individual strengths and weaknesses. **Note**: If you are using peer leaders to co-teach this course, let these peers take a lead when presenting this topic.

D. Suggested Outline for Addressing Topics in Chapter 2

STEP I: BEGIN WITH A LECTURE LAUNCHER OR ICEBREAKER ACTIVITY
STEP II: EMPLOY A VARIETY OF CLASSROOM ACTIVITIES
     a. Use PowerPoint presentation from *Multimedia Manager 2007* resource
     b. Expand on key lesson themes
     c. Involve peer leaders
     d. Use chapter exercises
     e. Engage students in learning through case studies
STEP III: REVIEW & PREVIEW
     a. Address common questions and concerns about the topic
     b. Writing reflection
     c. Prepare for next class

Expanded Lesson Plan

STEP I: Lecture Launchers and Icebreakers

- College students, especially freshman who may be away from home for the first time, may spend excessive amounts of time online. It's not inconceivable that students will spend more time on e-mail, instant messaging, and general Internet surfing than they do on their studies. After generating a discussion on how much of their time your students are using on online pursuits, you can segue into a dialogue about daily planning (i.e., building more structured Internet time into their schedule) or even procrastination (i.e., making sure that Internet time doesn't become a time-sucking distraction from their school work).

- When discussing time management principles, the phrase "work smarter, not harder" is often tossed around. But what does that mean, exactly? Figure 2.3 in the text is a blank Weekly Timetable chart that students were asked to complete as homework. Have them trade charts with a partner. After the students have examined each other's schedules, ask them to create a more time-effective plan for their partner. Then ask students to share what they've learned from the assignment. Hopefully, this will illustrate the principle of working smarter.

STEP II: Classroom Activities

a. Use the PowerPoint presentations in *Multimedia Manager 2007* to complement your mini lecture.

b. Key Lesson Themes

- **Goal Setting:** Use Exercise 2.1 to lead a discussion on goal setting. This general exercise asks students to name five goals they would like to set for themselves over the next decade. Next, they are asked to consider to measurable objectives for achieving those goals. Using this exercise helps reiterate what students have learned in Chapter 1, as well as impress upon them the importance of managing their time if they are to achieve their stated goals.

- **Scheduling:** This may be an appropriate time to discuss the "two for one" rule: students should plan to study two hours outside of class for every hour spent in class. Obviously, the true amount of time needed for each class can depend on the teacher's expectations and the student's previous knowledge, organization, and ability, and can vary considerably from week to week. But it is important early in the term for students to understand differences in expectations between high school and college, and that teachers who assign the equivalent of six hours of reading and homework per week for a three credit hour class are not overloading them. In high school, students spend six or seven hours per day in class; in college they may spend as few as two or three hours per day in class. It is important that as students plan their time, they acknowledge that they bear more responsibility for their own learning in college than they did in high school. Use Exercise 2.3: Tracking "Actual Time" to emphasize this point.

c. Group Activities

- Assign students into small groups of three or four. Within each group, assign roles. One will play the role of a student trying to study. The others should provide potential distractions – a roommate who wants to chat, a floor mate who stops by and invites the student out for a pizza, a phone call from an old friend. As a group, these students should work together to create a skit illustrating how the beleaguered students could gracefully (but firmly!) remove themselves from potentially distracting situations. Have each group perform their skits for the entire class. Then ask the class to critique each group's skits.

- An alternative to this is to have students perform their skits impromptu (i.e., improvise as soon as the roles are assigned). Emphasize that those playing the role of the distracter need to be persistent, as this will test the student's ability to say "no."

d. Peer Leader Assistance

- Using their syllabi from ALL of the courses they are taking this semester, have the students schedule their exams and assignment due dates in their personal Student Planner. This will be a nice resource for them to keep since it will allow them to see what papers and tests they have during any given week for the entire semester. You may give extra points for this.

- Be prepared to discuss how you make time for different things in your own life, including setting time aside to study. Give a testimonial on how good time management is a major reason for your success as a student.

- Show the students your method of time management (planner, daily schedule, etc.) and explain how these methods have been beneficial to you.

- Share with the class your strategies for coping when "the going gets tough." Be honest; explain how some stress-related situations could have been avoided. This would be a good time to remind students about the numerous support services that are available on campus.

e. Case Studies

Tina
Tina turns in her sample daily planner. It is filled in completely from 6:00 a.m. to 1:30 or 2:00 a.m. every day. As you read through it, you realize that this schedule is not an exaggeration. Tina commutes 75 minutes each way to attend classes. She is a single mother; her son and daughter are both in elementary school and are active in athletics, scout, and church activities. Tina works full time to support her family and pay for

school. She is taking 15 credit hours, including a laboratory science. Tina says she is so stressed out she is afraid she will never make it to final exams.

Discussion Questions:
1. How might you respond to Tina's concern that she will "never make it to final exams"?
2. What are some of the things that Tina can do to keep from feeling overwhelmed?
3. Are there any campus resources Tina can use to help ease her load?

Charlie

Charlie has always been a C student. Before coming to college, however, he decided that he was going to work harder and reach for higher grades. At first, his mission was successful. He studied mainly in the library, on a regular schedule, and used his planner to chart out and prioritize his "to do" list. Before long, Charlie was making A's and B's. But at a Halloween party, Charlie met Vanessa. The two hit it off and before long were practically inseparable. Charlie saw his grades decline. He knew he needed to get his studying back on track, but whenever he blocked off study time, Vanessa would either suggest that they study together (in which case, Charlie accomplished much less than when he studied alone) or go off and pout. Charlie wasn't sure what to do. He really liked Vanessa and didn't want to lose her, but he also didn't want to have to sacrifice his GPA for a girlfriend.

Discussion Questions:
1. What are some things Charlie could say to Vanessa to help her understand his situation?
2. How should Charlie handle Vanessa's pouting and suggestions that they study together instead of alone?
3. Should Charlie break up with Vanessa?

f. Chapter Exercises

- **Exercise 2.2: The Ideal Class Schedule**
  It may be preferable to return to this exercise later in the term when students are beginning to schedule advising appointments. This exercise reinforces students' responsibility to prepare for advising, and helps them understand that their ability to control their time during future academic terms is related to their advance planning as well as their assessment of their own preferences. Developing a class schedule that accommodates other commitments (e.g., work, family, commuting) can facilitate effective time management.

- **Exercise 2.4: Your Daily Plan**
  If students already maintain a planner (many have developed this habit in high school), consider giving them the option of photocopying a week from their planner and turning it in as an assignment. If the assignment is to be graded, specify what you want included (e.g., classes, appointments, obligations, items from their "to do" list). It can also be helpful to ask students to write an evaluation of the usefulness of their planner as they

currently use it and to brainstorm other ways that maintaining a planner can assist them in organizing and controlling their time.

STEP III: *Review and Preview*

REVIEW

a. Address Common Questions and Concerns of First-Year Students:

- *Why should I keep a written list of the things I need to do? I can remember everything in my head.*
  Answer: By creating a "to do" list, your students can prioritize the tasks they need to accomplish. They can also create a system of differentiating between academic assignments and personal errands, such as denoting each type a different color. And of course, every time they complete a task, they are rewarded with the satisfaction of being able to physically cross it off the list.

- *I know I am a procrastinator. Why should I do things any differently in college than I did in high school? I work best under pressure.*
  Answer: As the text explains, recent research indicates that procrastinators are more likely to develop unhealthy habits like higher alcohol consumption, smoking, insomnia, poor diet, and lack of exercise. Procrastination can also seep into other areas of a student's life, creating a pattern of avoidance. It is best to get these tendencies under control earlier rather than later, or else the student could begin to feel overwhelmed by their commitments.

- *How can I manage my time when my roommate is completely disorganized and keeps me up all night?*
  Answer: Encourage your students to create a plan for their living space. They could work with their roommate to set "quiet hours" for studying or sleeping. If the student is not on good terms with his/her roommate, or the roommate refuses to comply, the student could approach the resident assistant or hall director to help intervene. As a last resort, the student could apply for a room reassignment.

- *How am I supposed to find enough time to study when I have to work to pay my way through school (or play a collegiate sport, or create time for my family...)?*
  Answer: Impress upon your students that time management is key to juggling multiple commitments. Studying doesn't mean that they have to give up all non-academic pursuits. On the contrary, students who work or participate in sports often achieve higher grades than their less-active counterparts—due in part to the important role that time management plays in their lives. However, if your student is truly overloaded with commitments, and cannot reduce their load of responsibility, it may be time for that student to reassess whether or not right now is the time for their education.

b. Writing Reflection

Choose one or more of the reflection questions on page 40 in the text and ask students to respond in writing.

PREVIEW FOR NEXT CLASS

Students need to be reminded to take the Myers Briggs Personality Inventory before the next class. In addition, decide whether you want them to complete the Multiple Intelligences Inventory and the Vark Learning Styles Inventory before the next class and inform the students accordingly.

E. Test Questions

Multiple Choice - choose ONE answer per question.

1. Earning a 3.5 GPA is an example of what kind of goal?
   a. Lofty
   b. Unrealistic
   c. Measurable
   d. Civil

2. For each hour spent in class, you should schedule _____ hour(s) of study time.
   a. ½
   b. 1
   c. 1 ½
   d. 2

3. Two of the most cited differences between high school and college are increased autonomy and
   a. increased interdependence.
   b. greater responsibility.
   c. less responsibility.
   d. none of the above

4. The text recommends dividing study time into _____ blocks.
   a. 30-minute
   b. 45-minute
   c. 50-minute
   d. 60-minute

5. What is the most important reason to be on time for class?
   a. because it shows respect for both your professor and your classmates
   b. because it affects your class participation grade
   c. because your parents are paying for it
   d. because you might miss something you need to know for a test

6. It's hard to study on _____ stomach.
   a. an empty
   b. a full
   c. a and b
   d. none of the above

7. Procrastination is a_____
   a. learning style.
   b. serious problem.
   c. psychological disorder.
   d. none of the above

8. Recognizing what time of day or night you are most alert and engaged is learning about your
   a. learning style.
   b. biorhythms.
   c. psychological patterns.
   d. none of the above

9. Block-scheduling literally means
   a. back-to-back classes.
   b. 2-hr classes.
   c. classes once per week.
   d. none of the above

10. Time management is
    a. unattainable.
    b. a lifelong skill.
    c. only achieved by Type A students.
    d. none of the above

True/False

11. The chapter suggests that using a daily planner helps relieve stress.

12. The text recommends scheduling at least three aerobic workouts per week.

13. To achieve optimal results, it is recommended that you study your most difficult or most boring subjects first.

14. If you want to be successful, you should adhere strictly to your plans of action, regardless of what else is going on around you.

15. One way to beat procrastination is to break down large tasks into smaller steps.

Short Answer

16. Name three components of good time management.

17. Recent research indicates that students who are prone to procrastination are also at risk for what?

18. Name one benefit and one drawback to block scheduling.

19. List three ways to avoid distractions while studying.

20. Name one thing you can do to demonstrate basic politeness in the classroom.

Essay

21. What behaviors do you consider to be rude and disrespectful? What role can you play in enhancing civility in the classroom?

22. Describe the top five ways that you organize your day. What are the strengths and challenges of these methods/ways/behaviors?

23. Which principle of time management do you consider to be the most important? Why?

24. What is your ideal class schedule and why?

25. Which principle of time management is your least favorite? Why?

CHAPTER 2 ANSWER KEY

1. c, p. 21
2. d, p. 26
3. b, p. 21
4. c, p. 32
5. a, p. 36
6. c, p. 32
7. b, p. 24
8. b, p. 24
9. a, p. 34
10. b, p. 36
11. true, p. 26
12. true, p. 30
13. true, p. 32
14. true, p. 35
15. true, p. 30

16. Should include three of the following: knowing what your goals are, deciding where your priorities lie, anticipating future needs and possible changes, placing yourself in control of your time, making a commitment to being punctual, and carrying out your plans, p. 21
17. Avoiding other tasks and problems; more likely to develop unhealthy habits such as higher alcohol consumption, smoking, insomnia, poor diet, and lack of exercise, p. 25
18. Benefits include cutting travel time, providing more flexibility for scheduling employment or family commitments. Drawbacks include little time to process information or student between classes, fatigue, stress, too many exams or projects due on the same day, and each absence due to illness means missing all of your classes, instead of two or three.

F. Web Resources

Time Management Tips – http://www.gmu.edu/gmu/personal/time.html
George Mason University hosts this site, which gives instructions for taking a personal time survey as well as several useful ideas for better managing time.

Personal Goal Setting – http://www.time-management-guide.com/personal-goal-setting.html
This comprehensive site offers a wealth of information about personal goal setting, and how students can turn those goals into action plans.

Learn to Prioritize – http://www.suite101.com/article.cfm/17943/103703
Ask your students to read this article, which explains how learning to prioritize can reduce the level of stress in their lives, academic or otherwise.

Printable Checklists – http://www.allfreeprintables.com/checklists/to-do-lists.shtml
Direct your students to this site, where they can print out free to do lists. The site also offers free, printable checklists for other activities such as grocery shopping and childproofing your home.

Student Organizer – http://www.primasoft.com/so.htm
Some students may benefit from an electronic organizer, but cannot afford a PDA. In this case, direct them to the above link for PrimaSoft's Course Book software, which organizes everything from assignments to your own custom dictionary of terms. After a 30-day free trial, students who like the software may purchase it for a small fee (around $25).

Mastering Time 101 – http://members.aol.com/rslts/101Frames.html
This free, online seminar presents less conventional methods of time management, focusing on rethinking the concept of time.

Techniques to Manage Procrastination - www.ucc.vt.edu/stdysk/procrast.html, oregon.uoregon.edu/~gtistadt/procras.html

Hints for Planning Study Time - www.coun.uvic.ca/learn/program/hndouts/plan_ho.html

Mind Tools for Getting the Most out of Your Time – an index of articles – www.mindtools.com/page5.html.

Control of the Environment - www.ucc.vt.edu/stdysk/control.html

G. For More Information

Davidson, Jeff. (2001). *The complete idiot's guide to time management (3rd ed)*. New York: Alpha Books.

DeGraaf, John, ed. (2003). *Take back your time: Fighting overwork and time poverty in America*. San Francisco, CA: Berrett-Koehler Publishers.

Lagatree, Kirsten. (1999). *Checklists for life: 10l lists to help you get organized, save time, and unclutter your life*. New York: Random House Reference.

Merrill, A. Roger and Rebecca Merrill. (2003). *Life matters: Creating a dynamic balance of work, family, time, and money*. New York: McGraw-Hill.

Sapadin, Linda. (1999). *Beat procrastination and make the grade: The six styles of procrastination and how students can overcome them*. New York: Penguin.

Chapter 3: How We Learn

By Steven Blume, professor of English and Associate Dean of the McDonough Center for Leadership in Education and Business at Marietta College

Ideas for Instruction and Instructor Training	Video and CD-ROMs	Media Resources for Instructors	Media Resources for Students
Instructor's Manual (IM) Includes a brief lesson plan for Chapter 3, chapter objectives, lecture launchers, commentary on exercises in the book, and case studies. **Test Bank (in IM)** Multiple Choice, True/False, Short Answer and Essay Questions. Also available in ExamView® electronic format, which can be customized to fit your needs.	*10 Things Every Student Needs to Succeed in College* **Video** 6-minute segment entitled "Knowing Your Own Learning Styles." *10 Things Every Student Needs to Know to Study* **Video** 6-minute segment entitled "Learning Strategically." **ExamView® CD-ROM** Computerized version of the Test Bank items for Chapter 3.	JoinIn™ Hand-held audience response device allows students immediate response to multiple-choice questions, polls, and interactive exercises. **Multimedia Manager 2007 CD-ROM** PowerPoint presentations, video clips, images, and web links help with assembly, editing, and presentation of multimedia lectures.	**iLrn® Pin-Coded Website** Contains self-assessments, electronic journals that encourage students to reflect on their progress, essay questions and exercises, and Test Your Knowledge interactive quizzes for chapter 3. **InfoTrac® College Edition** May be bundled with text. *Keywords:* college success, liberal arts, goal setting, values, colleges, universities. **WebTutor™ Toolbox** Online course management tool for WebCT™ or Blackboard preloaded with text-specific content and media resources for Chapter 3.

A. Chapter Objectives

1. To introduce students to many approaches for understanding learning styles or preferences
2. To help students discover their own psychological type and learning styles
3. To teach students how to develop learning styles other than their own preferred style and to increase the flexibility of the way they study
4. To help students understand and recognize a learning disability

B. Timing of Chapter Coverage

For the sake of concentration of effort and continuity, teach this chapter soon after you have taught Chapter 2 on time management.

C. About This Chapter

This chapter can be valuable in showing students that study skills can be linked to an awareness of how they learn. If they know their strengths, they can develop study skills to help them compensate for their weaknesses. Simply having students read this chapter without doing the exercises will not really help them understand learning styles or broaden their own learning style. Some first-year students believe a mystery surrounds the success of some students and the failure of others - that there's a kind of magic that successful students have. You know this isn't true. By teaching study skills in general and addressing learning styles, you can help

- demystify success and failure.
- provide a series of methods that will encourage being a more deliberate and organized student.
- facilitate the students' self-development.

Demystification

The opening section of this chapter suggests that many first-year students do believe there is a mysterious process at work. A student does well in one course that is primarily done in lecture mode and thinks classroom discussions are a waste of time, while his roommate thinks just the opposite.

Deliberateness

If your students know that classes are not simply chaotic, they should be able to approach learning somewhat more deliberately than they might have without this knowledge. Teaching learning styles is another way you can reinforce one of the basic premises of *Your College Experience*—that college success depends largely on careful planning.

Self-Development

The section on learning styles and personality types suggests that as first-year students develop, they will need to expand their learning styles. This is just another way of adding to their "bag of tricks." As a writing instructor used to tell her students in response to their complaints that she was trying to destroy their writing styles, "I'm not trying to destroy your styles at all; I'm trying to help you develop a variety of styles."

D. Suggested Outline for Discussing Chapter 3

STEP I: BEGIN WITH A LECTURE LAUNCHER OR ICEBREAKER ACTIVITY
STEP II: EMPLOY A VARIETY OF CLASSROOM ACTIVITIES
    a. Use the PowerPoint presentation from *Multimedia Manager 2007* resource
    b. Expand on key lesson themes
    c. Involve peer leaders
    d. Use chapter exercises
    e. Engage students in learning through case studies
STEP III: REVIEW & PREVIEW
    a. Address common questions and concerns about the topic
    b. Writing reflection
    c. Prepare for next class

Expanded Lesson Plan

STEP I: Lecture Launchers and Icebreakers

- Use these instructions to present an exercise that focuses on the different ways people acquire information. Follow the script and directions with the class:

"I am going to ask you as a class to all do one action and then freeze. Are you ready? Do this and then freeze. Look at your fingernails. Leave your hands frozen and look up at me. Now use one of your hands to raise your hand to respond to one of these questions. How many held out your hands, palm down, fingers pointed away, looking at your nails and the back of your hand?" (Drawn on the board a rough figure of a hand and fingers extended. Draw in the nails.)

"Raise your hand if you did this." (Demonstrate.) Count the number and write it on the board by the figure. "Thank you. Hands down."

"Now, how many curled your fingers back over your palm and looked at your nails?" (Draw this figure.) "Raise your hand if you did this." (Demonstrate.) Count this number and write it on the board. "Thank you. Hands down."

"Finally, how many of you just looked at your fingernails without moving your hands at all?" Count again and write this number on the board. "Okay, unfreeze."

"Here I am, your instructor. I asked my class to do a simple task, and I got different responses. What suggestions can you give me?" From here, the discussion can follow in many directions such as how we all differ, how you might differ from your instructor, and different personality types. A student may ask,

"What is the right answer?" This opens up discussion that many questions in college classes may not have only one answer. You can explain to the students that faculty may be more interested in how a student arrived at the answer, no matter what it is.

Exercise written by C. B. Red Bright, Jackson State Community College, Jackson, TN

- Ask students to jot down on a scrap of paper their answer to this question: "A meeting scheduled for 10:30 has been moved up 30 minutes. What time does the meeting start?" Pause for a moment and then repeat, "Moved up 30 minutes. What time does the meeting start?" Count the answers for both 10:00 and 11:00. Again, discuss the differences with your students. Have the differing "sides" defend their answers. Tell them it all hinges on the word "up" in time. Encourage students to analyze why "up" in time means that to them. Don't accept, "That's just want it means." Emphasize importance of vocabulary and of asking teachers for clarification when necessary.

STEP II: Classroom Activities

a. Use the PowerPoint presentations in *Multimedia Manager 2007* to complement your mini lecture.

b. Key Lesson Themes

- Give a short explanation of the Experimental Learning Model. Allow students to express their understanding of this model.

- Develop a lesson on the Myers Briggs Types. Explain the meaning of the letters.

c. Group Activities

- To participate in this exercise, your students must have already done the MBTI and know the four letters of their learning style; for example, INTP, INFJ. At the beginning of the exercise, ask students to write their four-letter type on an index card that you provide and tape it to their shirts. Group students into pairs representing opposites: S/I (sensing/intuition) types together and T/F (thought/feeling) types together. Present an out-of-class assignment to be completed for the next class period. This assignment should involve information gathering rather than personal experience; for example, a short analysis of the current struggles in Iraq. When the students come to the next class, they should be prepared to participate in a discussion of the answers to the assigned questions. You need to be prepared to keep the discussion focused on learning styles.

d. Peer Leader Assistance

- The following tasks will help students analyze and adjust to the different teaching styles of their instructors, to develop learning styles other than their own preferred style (i.e. less dominant learning style), and to increase the flexibility of the way they study:

  o Discuss your learning style and how you have adapted to professors who teach in different styles.
  o Offer strategies on how students could adapt to a professor whose teaching style does not match their (the students') learning styles.
  o Make a list of the preferred learning style of each student. Keep for further classroom assignments.

e. Case Studies

Keisha

Keisha is a first-year student taking 15 credits. She has found out that there is a lot of work required for each class. She also sees that instructors seem to have a different way of teaching their class and emphasizing the material. Keisha seems to be having the most trouble with her Philosophy class and is finding the lecture hard to follow. She got a D on the first test and is worried because she was a good student in high school. The professor discusses many aspects of the different philosophers' theories during the lecture. Keisha is having difficulty tying them together and is more in tune with the names of key figures, dates, and major points. Her next test is in two weeks.

Discussion Questions:
1. Why is Keisha having this difficulty?
2. What can she do to improve her situation?
3. What can Keisha do to better understand each lecture?
4. How can Keisha best prepare for her next exam?

Howie

Howie's lab partner, Kai, has a particular way of completing each assignment. She is thorough and methodical, and seems to have an immediate grasp of all new material they are learning in class. Howie, however, needs more time to digest the concepts they're studying. Kai becomes very critical and impatient with Howie whenever he asks her a question. Clearly, Kai prefers working by herself than with another person. As a result, Kai often completes the assignments with little input from Howie. Howie feels that Kai's interference keeps him from fully learning the material covered by each lab assignment. His mother has suggested he speak to his professor about this problem, but Howie doesn't want to sound like a complainer.

Discussion Questions:
1. What psychological types would you assess to both Howie and Kai?

2. How could Howie work with his learning style to improve his relationship with Kai?
3. If you were Howie, what would you do: go to your professor or work things out with Kai on your own?

f. Chapter Exercises

- **Exercise 3.1: Myers-Briggs Exploration**
  After forming small groups in class, assign them to do this exercise on their own time and then present the results to the class as a whole. This not only gives them the time they need to complete the project, but also fosters familiarity outside of the classroom.

- **Exercise 3.2: Learning Styles Models**
  This is yet another exercise that promotes good classroom discussion.

- **Exercise 3.3: Learning about Learning Disabilities**
  This exercise should be done at home. Again, this would be a good exercise for class discussion after they have completed work in groups.

STEP III: Review and Preview

REVIEW

a. Address Common Questions and Concerns of First-Year Students:

- *How can you put people in these little boxes?*
  Answer: Students should be encouraged to understand psychological types. Have them try the self-assessment on page 44 to see where they stand.

- *I'm eighteen years old. How can I change my learning style now?*
  Answer: Encourage students to work on their strengths while exploring other learning styles.

- *Is one learning style better than another?*
  Answer: The book does not try to privilege any one style over the other. However, students should be aware of the preferred learning styles for acquiring information to be a doctor, lawyer, or teacher.

- *Why do I really need to develop a wider range of learning styles?*
  Answer: In order for college to work, students will need a great variety of skills. Really emphasize the importance of sensing, analytical, auditory, and other learning styles.

- *Will my learning style really be relevant to anything after I graduate from college?*
  Answer: Stress to your students that they are developing life-long skills.

- *What difference do learning styles make in job situations?*
  Answer: Just as groups can be enhanced with people who have different learning styles, so can the work place.

b. Writing Reflection

- Choose one or more of the reflection questions on page 62 in the text and ask students to respond in writing.

PREVIEW FOR NEXT CLASS

You might want to give your students Exercise 4.3 as an outside class assignment to prepare them for the next class topic. Or, you might want to consider asking students to do a search on the topic of active learning, using library and Internet resources. Ask each student to bring in just one benefit of active learning from such a search.

E. Test Questions

Multiple Choice - choose ONE answer per question.

1. There is/are _____ learning style models
   a. only one
   b. two
   c. five
   d. numerous

2. The S/N (sensing/intuition) preference scale describes how you
   a. acquire information.
   b. make decisions.
   c. study.
   d. none of the above

3. The T/F (thinking/feeling) preference scale describes how you
   a. acquire information.
   b. think.
   c. make decisions.
   d. none of the above

4. One weakness of someone with a thinking learning style is that he/she tends to
    a. make decisions with insufficient data.
    b. be less organized.
    c. not notice people's feelings.
    d. none of the above

5. One strength of someone with a sensing style is that he/she
    a. is not judgmental.
    b. attends to detail.
    c. works alone.
    d. none of the above

6. Your learning style reflects
    a. your intelligence.
    b. how hard you study.
    c. the way you acquire knowledge.
    d. none of the above

7. Field independent learners tend to
    a. be highly autonomous.
    b. require a lot of interaction.
    c. choose areas of study like the humanities.
    d. none of the above

8. According to Kolb, effective learners need _____ different kinds of abilities.
    a. five
    b. six
    c. seven
    d. none of the above

9. Extraverts tend to be
    a. gregarious.
    b. talkative.
    c. a and b
    d. none of the above

10. The theory of multiple intelligences was developed in 1983 by
    a. Dr. John Gardner.
    b. Dr. Howard Gardner.
    c. a and b
    d. none of the above

True/False

11. According to the Kolb Inventory of Learning Styles, if you are a *converger*, you like the world of ideas and theories.

12. The abilities that are characteristic of assimilators are of value to all students; especially those in the arts.

13. An instructor who asks you to critically analyze essays probably has a sensing learning style.

14. Learning styles and teaching styles are always in conflict.

15. Research shows that all human beings have at least eight different types of intelligence.

Short Answer

16. What does the term "psychological type" refer to specifically?

17. Your psychological type is the combination of your preferences on what four different scales?

18. What does the acronym VARK mean?

19. In what ways do individuals with Sensing and Intuition take in ideas differently?

20. In what ways do individuals with Judging and Perceiving make decisions and judgments differently?

Essay

21. Imagine a world in which everyone had the same learning style as you. How would life be better? How might it be worse? Explain your answers fully.

22. Where do you think you fall on the Myers-Briggs Personality Type Indicator? What characteristics do you exhibit that lead to your conclusion? Is your "type" evident in how you are experiencing your different classes? In what ways?

23. How can knowing your VARK score help you do better in your college classes? Now that you know your VARK score, what changes do you propose to make in how you study and why?

24. Identify one of your present instructors whose teaching style conflicts with your learning style. Outline in detail some changes that you plan to make to insure that you make a good grade in this class.

25. If you suspect you have a learning disability, develop a plan of action on how you will address this and insure that you make a good GPA your first semester in college.

Chapter 3 Answer Key

1. d, p. 45
2. a, p. 49
3. c, p. 50
4. c, p. 49
5. b, p. 49
6. a, p. 45
7. a, p. 45
8. d, p. 46
9. c, p. 48
10. b, p. 51
11. true, p. 47
12. false, p. 47
13. false, p. 50
14. false, p. 56
15. true, p. 52
16. the personality theory of Carl Gustav Jung, p. 47
17. extraversion vs. introversion, sensing vs. intuition, thinking vs. feeling, and judging vs. perceiving. Also acceptable: inner or outer world, facts or ideas, logic or values, organization or adaptability, pp. 48-50
18. Visual, Auditory, Read/Write, and Kinesthetic. p. 54

F. Web Resources

Myers Briggs Personality Inventory – http://similarminds.com/myers-briggs.html
You can direct your students to this site, which offers a free MBTI test you can use in the Additional Exercises listed in this chapter of the Instructor's Resource Manual Suite.

Temperament Sorter – http://www.advisorteam.com/temperament_sorter/register.asp?partid=1
This version of the Keirsey Temperament Sorter is partially free (it reveals ½ the results), but it is a fairly accurate online tool. If your students would like to know their full types, they may purchase an in-depth report for a small fee (around $15). The site also offers discounts to instructors.

Index of Learning Styles Questionnaire – http://www.engr.ncsu.edu/learningstyles/ilsweb.html
The ILS offered on this page was authored by Barbara A. Solomon and Richard M. Felder. It is entirely free and is accompanied by pages explaining the different styles assessed by this questionnaire – a good alternative to the Keirsey link above.

Relationships – http://www.literacynet.org/lp/learn2learn/students/relationships.html
For students interested in knowing more about how their learning styles affect their relationships, this site offers bulleted lists of qualities common among types, as well as strengths and challenges for each individual.

Teaching Style Inventory – http://www.teacherinventory.net/
Consider sharing the results of this inventory with your students to facilitate a discussion about how learning styles affect both students and teachers.

On Learning Styles – http://www.gsu.edu/~dschjb/wwwmbti.html
Georgia State University's master teaching program offers this extensive document, which offers several strategies for teaching each different type of student.

Field Independence/Dependence and Other Styles of Learning/Cognition -
www.lincoln.ac.nz/educ/tip/81.htm

Index of Learning Styles (Assessment) and Other Information on Learning Styles -
www2.ncsu.edu/unity/lockers/users/f/felder/public/ILSpage.html

Assessment of Learning Modalities (Visual, Auditory, Tactile/Kinesthetic) -
www.hcc.hawaii.edu/intranet/committees/FacDevCom/guidebk/teachtip/lernstyl.htm

Study Distraction Analysis - www.ucc.vt.edu/stdysk/studydis.html

G. For More Information

Avila, Alexander. (1999). *Lovetypes: Discover your romantic style and find your soul mate.* New York: Avon.

Keirsey, David. (1998). *Please understand me II: Temperament, character, and intelligence.* Del Mar, CA: Prometheus Nemesis.

Lawrence, Gordon D. (1997). *Looking at type and learning styles.* Gainesville, FL: Center for Applications of Psychological Type.

Myers, Isabel Briggs and Peter Myers. (1993). *Gifts differing: Understanding personality type.* Palo Alto, CA: Consulting Psychologists Press.

Tieger, Paul D. and Barbara Barron-Tieger. (2001). *Do what you are: Discover the perfect career for you through the secrets of personality type (3rd ed).* New York: Little, Brown & Company.

Chapter 4: Engagement with Learning

Ideas for Instruction and Instructor Training	Videos and CD-ROMs	Media Resources for Instructors	Media Resources for Students
Instructor's Manual (IM) Includes a brief lesson plan for Chapter 4, chapter objectives, lecture launchers, commentary on exercises in the book, and case studies. **Test Bank (in IM)** Multiple Choice, True/False, Short Answer and Essay Questions. Also available in ExamView® electronic format, which can be customized to fit your needs.	***10 Things Every Student Needs to Know to Study Video*** 6-minute segment entitled "Learning in the Classroom." **ExamView® CD-ROM** Computerized version of the Test Bank items for Chapter 4.	**JOININ™** Hand-held audience response device allows students immediate response to multiple-choice questions, polls, and interactive exercises. **Multimedia Manager 2007 CD-ROM** PowerPoint presentations, video clips, images, and web links help with assembly, editing, and presentation of multimedia lectures.	**iLrn® Pin-Coded Website** Contains self-assessments, electronic journals that encourage students to reflect on their progress, essay questions and exercises, and Test Your Knowledge interactive quizzes for chapter 4. **InfoTrac® College Edition** May be bundled with text. *Keywords:* college success, liberal arts, goal setting, values, colleges, universities. **WebTutor™ Toolbox** Online course management tool for WebCT™ or Blackboard preloaded with text-specific content and media resources for Chapter 4.

A. Chapter Objectives

1. To explain what engaged learning means and why it is important
2. To clarify the differences between high school and college
3. To justify the use of active learning in the college classroom
4. To demonstrate—by example—that active learning makes learning more enjoyable
5. To help students realize that a positive relationship with an instructor may be a critical part of the learning process in college
6. To explain what college teachers expect of their students

B. Timing of Chapter Coverage

Cover the specifics of time management (Chapter 2) before approaching this chapter. You may also consider tackling the chapters on note-taking, reading, and studying before beginning this chapter.

C. About This Chapter

There is an abundance of research and scholarship to support the importance of actively involving students in the learning process. This chapter provides for students a rationale for the value of becoming engaged in the learning process and offers strategies to accomplish this. Since the authors believe so completely in active learning, we recommend that as instructors you strive to employ as many active learning devices as you can throughout the first-year seminar course:

- Ask students for feedback regularly, read their remarks, and respond to them.

- Employ the "one-minute paper" at the end of class: What was the most important issue of today's class? What is the unanswered question you have about today's class? The answers will prepare you to reach your students the next day.

- Encourage students to get to know their teachers. A suggestion: challenge each student to interview the teacher he or she likes least. Students may only confirm their dislike in some cases, but in others they may find a different individual sitting across the desk from them.

- Help students understand that there are no "dumb questions." Challenge them to ask the questions that nobody else in the room wants to ask because they think the instructor will laugh at them, even though they need answers.

D. Suggested Outline for Addressing Topics in Chapter 4

STEP I: BEGIN WITH A LECTURE LAUNCHER OR ICEBREAKER ACTIVITY
STEP II: EMPLOY A VARIETY OF CLASSROOM ACTIVITIES
    a. Use the PowerPoint presentation from *Multimedia Manager 2007* resource
    b. Expand on key lesson themes
    c. Involve peer leaders
    d. Use chapter exercises
    e. Engage students in learning through case studies
STEP III: REVIEW & PREVIEW
    a. Address common questions and concerns about the topic
    b. Writing reflection
    c. Prepare for next class

Expanded Lesson Plan

STEP I: Lecture Launchers and Icebreakers

- Ask your students to write a response to this question: "What is engagement with learning?" Take the time to have students read their answers to the rest of the class. It will be time well spent. You will learn if they understand the difference, and you'll probably be able to elaborate on some of the comments they make. This activity could serve as a segue into the lesson mini lecture.

- Share some of the **personal distresses** that you encountered as you made the transition from high school to college. Let the students offer suggestions on how things have changed or are similar from when you were a freshman to now.

STEP II: *Classroom Activities*

a. Use the PowerPoint presentations in *Multimedia Manager 2007* to complement your mini lecture.

b. Key Lesson Themes

- Expectations often differ between students and faculty. Students may be surprised by the expectations of their instructors. Some are even taken "off guard" and can be resistant. Open a dialogue between you and the class about these expectations. You can start by discussing the background, qualities, and expectations of a good teacher and a good student. During the discussion, point out some critical thinking and active learning skills that students bring to a situation where there is engagement in the learning process.

- Introduce your students to the chart in **Figure 4.2** (p. 67). Ask your students to use this as a sample to develop their own development hexagon. Have them write the same seven words in the appropriate places. Under each label, ask them to record some goals they plan to achieve that relate to that word. When they have finished, ask them to evaluate their hexagon. Which areas are full of goals? Which have just a few goals? Which are blank?

c. Group Activities

- You may consider having your students compare their hexagon with those of others. Encourage them to find a partner who might help them with a few of their goals, just as they might help another class member with his or her goals. Point out to students that another way to keep track of their development in this course is through the journal assignments at the end of each chapter. Suggest that they might want to consider using the seven terms of the hexagon to organize their thoughts. The objective here is to encourage students to evaluate their strengths and identify their weaknesses and to show students how strengthening active learning skills can lead to academic success.

d. Peer Leader Assistance

- Spend some time explaining to students the difference between helpful collaboration (working together openly on a project, seeking criticism from others, etc.) and illegal cheating (having someone else write a paper for you, getting quiz answers in advance, plagiarizing material, etc.).

e. Case Studies

Joseph

Joe is a student in his first year of college. In his science lab, he was placed in a group of three other students, all of whom are returning students and much older than he is. Joe's group decided together on task assignments and agreed to meet twice during the week to prepare. During the project, Joe attempted to contact the group repeatedly but the members could not agree on a time to meet due to their various other commitments. It is now two days before the due date for the project, and Joe has done very little work. One other group member finally calls him to tell him that everyone else has completed their tasks and they have decided on the plan for the class presentation. Joe is upset and tells the group member that he has not finished his part of the project because he was planning on the group meetings to help guide him. The group member suggests that Joe should not get any credit at all.

Discussion Questions:
1. What should Joe do to resolve this conflict?
2. How should Joe approach his group members? His instructor?
3. How could this problem have been avoided?
4. What are the benefits and pitfalls of collaborative learning in this situation?

Kelsea

Kelsea is an extremely bright first-year student. She routinely turns in A-level work to her instructors. The problem is that Kelsea rarely turns her work in on time, and is always asking for extensions. She blames her tardiness on insomnia, which she's suffered from since she was a young teen. Kelsea's insomnia has gotten so bad that she's begun missing classes due to sheer exhaustion. Through one particularly bad spell, Kelsea blows an important deadline on a research paper for her English instructor. The instructor's syllabus clearly states that late papers are not accepted, and if Kelsea gets a zero on this assignment, she will fail the class.

Discussion Questions:
1. If you were Kelsea, how would you handle this situation?
2. What would you do if you were Kelsea's instructor?
3. Is it fair for an instructor to bend the rules for a student in certain circumstances?

f. Chapter Exercises

- **Exercise 4.1: To Collaborate or Not?**
  Have your students complete this exercise after finishing a group project.

- **Exercise 4.2: Forming Your Ideal Learning Team**
  Because this exercise is about other members of the class, it is recommended that students complete this assignment outside of class.

- **Exercise 4.3: Learning about a Liberal Education**
  As suggested in the previous chapter, students can complete this exercise as a preparation for today's class.

- **Exercise 4.4: Differences between High School and College**
  You could adapt this exercise to accompany Exercise 4.5 by asking your students to size up their high school teachers in the same fashion they've evaluated their college instructors. Then, either in small groups or individually, have your students complete this exercise.

- **Exercise 4.5: Sizing Up Your College Teachers**
  When students have completed this exercise, have a discussion with the class, asking them what qualities their favorite teachers had in common.

STEP III: Review and Preview

REVIEW

a. Address Common Questions and Concerns of First-Year Students:

- *What can I do if I can't stand my teacher?*
  Answer: Express to your students the importance of meeting with their instructors during office hours. If this doesn't improve the situation, and it's early enough in the semester, they may want to exercise the "drop/add" option and find another class. But if that date has passed, and the situation still isn't resolved, it's time for your student to visit the department head. If the student remains unsatisfied with the outcome of that meeting, he or she should continue to climb the administrative ladder until they feel their voice has been heard.

- *Why don't teachers just tell me what I need to know, like they did in high school?*
  Answer: This is the sort of question that leads into a great discussion about the benefits of active learning versus those of passive learning. Most high school classrooms emphasize the latter, and that is what many students are more comfortable with. Review with your students the bullet points on page 71 that outline why active learning puts them in charge of their own education.

- *My friend is taking the same course from another teacher and the class is entirely different, not to mention easier. Why?*
  Answer: The courses seem different because every teacher is different. What's important is focusing on what and how you're learning in this particular course.

- *I need to make an appointment with my professor but he's never available. What can I do?*

Answer: If your professor's office hours conflict with your schedule, ask him to meet with you at an alternate time. If that doesn't work, see if you can set up a phone appointment. Another alternative is to e-mail your professor and open up a dialogue with him over the Internet. If you've tried all of the above and still can't arrange an appointment with your professor—i.e., if you've put out a good faith effort and he hasn't—it may be time to approach his department chair about his unwillingness to meet with you outside of class.

- ***When I try to ask my teacher why I'm doing so poorly on assignments, she doesn't seem to want to help me. What can I do about it?***
  Answer: First, evaluate how you're asking for help. Are you trying to get your teacher to spoon-feed you answers? It's likely that what you're interpreting as a lack of help on your teacher's part is her way of trying to get you to be more of an active learner, instead of a passive one. However, if you're honestly stumped as to how to do better on assignments, think about how you can phrase your questions to your teacher so that she understands you're not asking her to give you the answers. Asking about the process of arriving at the final product, instead of the final product itself, will show her that you're seeking comprehension, and not just an A.

b. Writing Reflection

- **The One-Minute Paper**

  1. Ask your students to choose one of their classes and write what they thought the main issue was that day. Tell them they should also list any unanswered questions they have for the next class.
  2. During the next class they attend, have them evaluate if those questions are now answered. If not, see if they can identify what active learning skills they can use to improve this situation.
  3. Consider asking your students to try this for a week. Then, ask them if this helped them master the information in the class and how.
  4. Students can write a summary of their experience as well as discuss it in class.

PREVIEW FOR NEXT CLASS

Make copies of a newspaper or magazine article on a social issue and distribute to the class. Ask your students to read the article before they come to the next class. In addition, they are to look critically at the content. Is there a bias? Did the author approach the subject with an open mind? Are there assumptions or conclusions that do not seem accurate? At the next class bring in an opinion piece to show students the difference.

E. Test Questions

Multiple Choice - choose ONE answer per question.

1. Engagement means
   a. active involvement in every aspect of life.
   b. approaching every challenge with determination.
   c. a and b
   d. none of the above

2. According to the text, when forming a learning team, you should NOT
   a. seek peers who are different than you in terms of cultural background.
   b. keep the group large (7 or more students).
   c. hold individual team members accountable for their own learning.
   d. hold individual team members accountable for contributing to the learning of their teammates.

3. If you need help from an instructor on an assignment, it is BEST to
   a. ask the instructor during the first five minutes of class.
   b. ask the instructor at the end of class.
   c. go see the instructor during office hours.
   d. send the instructor an e-mail.

4. In identifying a possible mentor, look for someone who
   a. takes a special interest in you.
   b. encourages you to challenge yourself.
   c. offers to meet with you to discuss your work.
   d. all of the above

5. About _____% of all students spend no time on physical fitness.
   a. 10
   b. 20
   c. 30
   d. 40

6. Simply put, academic freedom means that college teachers
   a. can speak their minds without fear of retribution.
   b. can force you to agree with their views.
   c. have the freedom to keep you after class if their lecture runs long.
   d. believe in the right of individuals to be free.

7. In a ground breaking study on factors predicting success in calculus, it was determined that the most effective strategy for success in calculus turned out to be
   a. active participation in a study group.

    b. individualized learning.

    c. a and b

    d. none of the above

8. If you are unsatisfied with a grade you received on a recent paper, the first thing you should do is

    a. file a complaint within the department.

    b. ask your teacher if you can redo the assignment.

    c. ask another instructor within the same department to look at your paper and offer a second opinion.

    d. speak with your teacher about why you received the grade you did.

9. When forming a learning team,

    a. include people who are just like you.

    b. ask your teacher to form your team.

    c. keep the group size large.

    d. remember that learning teams are more than study groups.

10. If you disagree with what your instructors say,

    a. politely challenge him or her.

    b. file a report with the administration.

    c. a and b

    d. none of the above

True/False

11. In a major study of teaching at Harvard University, one example for improving learning was a simple feedback exercise.

12. Competition is a key ingredient to collaborative learning.

13. You learn from your fellow classmates as well as from your instructors.

14. Academic freedom is a twenty-first century trend.`

15. Only tenured professors make good mentors.

Short Answer

16. Name three benefits of active learning.

17. According to the hexagon figure from the text, what are the different aspects of student development?

18. What are the two components of the one-minute paper?

19. What are some qualities you need to look for when choosing a mentor?

20. List some simple things you can do to improve relations between you and your teachers.

Essay

21. Collaborating with your peers to form learning teams is a powerful way to improve your own learning. However, many students think that forming a "study group" is the one and only type of learning team. Cite three other types of learning teams and explain why each may be particularly effective for improving your academic performance.

22. Think of a time when you've had a conflict with a teacher. What was the conflict? What was your role in it? The teacher's role? How was the conflict resolved? Is there anything you would do differently today?

23. Think of a time when you worked in a group to complete a project. What were some of the things that went wrong. If you had an opportunity to redo that project, what would you do differently?

24. The next time you are assigned a project that calls for a learning team, use at least four of the team learning "uses" that are highlighted on page 69. Document each activity; ranking your most to least favorite activity.

25. Identify someone you would like to be your mentor. Interview him or her and write an essay on why you chose this person and what you've learned about this person.

CHAPTER 4 ANSWER KEY
1. c, p. 64
2. b, p. 68
3. c, p. 71
4. d, p. 74
5. b, p. 65
6. a, p. 73
7. d, p. 74
8. d, p. 74
9. d, p. 68
10. a, p.67
11. true, p. 67
12. false, p. 68
13. true, p. 71
14. false, p. 73
15. false, p. 73

16. Should include three of the following: work with others, improve your critical thinking, listening, writing, and speaking skills, function independently and teach yourself, manage your time, gain sensitivity to cultural differences, p. 66
17. Cultural, Emotional, Intellectual, Physical, Social, Spiritual, and Vocational, p. 67
18. What was the main issue of that class and any unanswered questions you have, p. 67

F. Web Resources

Active v. Passive Learning - http://lpc1.clpccd.cc.ca.us/lpc/hanna/learning/activevspassive.htm
Have your students look at this grid, which outlines some of the differences between students who are passive and those who are learning actively. Afterward, they can take "How to Learn in College," a quiz found at http://lpc1.clpccd.cc.ca.us/lpc/hanna/learning/collegelearningquiz.htm.

How Is College Different? – http://www.smu.edu/alec/transition.html
Have your students take a look at this site, which defines high school as a "teaching environment" and college as a "learning environment." It contains several links to further comparisons between high school and college.

Making Friends with Instructors – http://www.adultstudent.com/student/share/bclark.html
AdultStudents.com offers this brief article, which offers tips for fostering a positive student-teacher relationship.

College Freedom – http://www.collegefreedom.org/
This "Website for Academic Freedom" is a clearinghouse for links to information on everything from academic freedom and professors to freedom of the college press.

Model of Active Learning –
http://www.hcc.hawaii.edu/intranet/committees/FacDevCom/guidebk/teachtip/active.htm
This model takes a look at four components of active learning – experience of doing, experience of observing, dialogue with self, and dialogue with others – and explains each component fully.

The One-Minute Paper – http://www.indiana.edu/~econed/issues/v29_1/1.htm
The *Journal of Economic Education* originally published this study, which looks at some empirical findings regarding the usefulness of the one-minute paper. The link takes you to an abstract of the article, but you can download the full report free from the site.

Subject-Specific Study Techniques -

City College of San Francisco Learning Assistance Center Favorite Academic Websites
http://www.ccsf.edu/Services/Learning_Assistance/favorites1.shtml

Chemeketa Community College Study Skills Resources: How to Study
http://studyweb.chemek.cc.or.us/resources.htm#How to Study

Startribune.com: Homework Help
http://www.startribune.com/homework_help/

Academic Resource Core LINKS: Study Skills
http://www.geocities.com/arc_links/links_4.htm?#skill

G. For More Information

Buckley, William F. Jr. (1978). *God & man at Yale: The superstitions of academic freedom.* Washington D.C.: Regnery Publishing.

Evans, Nancy J. (1998). *Student development in college: Theory, research, and practice.* San Francisco, CA: Jossey-Bass.

McKeachie, Wilbert et al. (2002). *McKeachie's teaching tips: Strategies, research, and theory for college and university teachers (11th ed).* Boston, MA: Houghton Mifflin.

Smith, Barbara Leigh and John McCann, eds. (2001). *Reinventing ourselves: Interdisciplinary education, collaborative learning, and experimentation in higher education.* Bolton, MA: Anker Pub. Co.

Spoden, Jeff. (1999). *To honor a teacher: Students pay tribute to their most influential mentors.* Kansas City, KS: Andrews McMeel Publishing.

Chapter 5: Critical Thinking

Ideas for Instruction and Instructor Training	Videos and CD-ROMs	Media Resources for Instructors	Media Resources for Students
Instructor's Manual (IM) Includes a brief lesson plan for Chapter 5, chapter objectives, lecture launchers, commentary on exercises in the book, and case studies. **Test Bank (in IM)** Multiple Choice, True/False, Short Answer and Essay Questions. Also available in ExamView® electronic format, which can be customized to fit your needs.	***10 Things Every Student Needs to Succeed in College* Video** 6-minute segment entitled "Think Critically." **ExamView® CD-ROM** Computerized version of the Test Bank items for Chapter 5.	**JOININ™** Hand-held audience response device allows students immediate response to multiple-choice questions, polls, and interactive exercises. **Multimedia Manager 2007 CD-ROM** PowerPoint presentations, video clips, images, and web links help with assembly, editing, and presentation of multimedia lectures.	**iLrn® Pin-Coded Website** Contains self-assessments, electronic journals that encourage students to reflect on their progress, essay questions and exercises, and Test Your Knowledge interactive quizzes for chapter 5. **InfoTrac® College Edition** May be bundled with text. *Keywords:* college success, liberal arts, goal setting, values, colleges, universities. **WebTutor™ Toolbox** Online course management tool for WebCT™ or Blackboard preloaded with text-specific content and media resources for Chapter 5.

A. Chapter Objectives

1. To define and illustrate critical thinking
2. To explain how college encourages critical thinking
3. To identify and explain four aspects of critical thinking
4. To clarify the difference between critical arguments and emotional ones
5. To demonstrate the importance of critical thinking beyond college

B. Timing of Chapter Coverage

We recommend that you spend time early in the term helping students understand the differences between high school and college thinking. Some first-year students already may have been exposed to such a process, but it's still worth emphasizing; much of what college success depends on is the ability to work through ideas as opposed to memorizing a series of facts. If we want college graduates to be effective and experienced critical thinkers, the habit of critical thinking needs to be established early in the college experience so that it can be repeatedly practiced, refined, and developed throughout the remaining college years. John Chaffee is director for the Center for Critical Thinking at La Guardia Community College and author of the book *Thinking Critically*. He points out the importance of introducing the development of critical thinking skills at the beginning of the college experience:

Becoming a critical thinker is a complex developmental process. This process is best grounded in a meaningful and coherent introduction to the field of Critical Thinking. Once established, this intellectual foundation can be further elaborated through students' coursework and reflection on their own on-going experiences (1994, p. 8).

The first-year seminar can help students develop critical thinking from the very beginning of college. Give students permission to voice their most absurd ideas without fear of criticism. Show how any idea must first be weighed against evidence before it is discarded. Stress the relationship of critical thinking, not only to writing and speaking, but to most things that crop up in their daily lives: choosing what to do on a weekend, deciding on a field of study, planning a vacation, or repairing a car.

C. About This Chapter

The following information can help you introduce your students to the practice of critical thinking, making sure that they have a strong grasp on it as a concept before plunging into the text. The instructional strategies may be used to teach a particular course unit on critical thinking, or they may be used throughout the semester across different course topics. For maximum effect, these strategies should be introduced within the context of an instructional unit devoted exclusively to critical thinking. Then students can use them to practice and reinforce critical thinking skills with respect to different course topics.

Scholars differ in their definitions of critical thinking. We define critical thinking as any thought process "higher" than rote learning of factual information. When students think critically, they not only know the facts, but they go beyond the facts and think about them in a different way from how those facts have been presented to them in class or in the text. Critical thinking involves reflecting on the information received, moving from "surface" learning toward "deep" learning, and from learning by "transmission" of knowledge by the teacher or text to learning by "transformation" of knowledge by the learner.

Critical thinking begins with active learning, but it goes further. For instance, writing out accurate and comprehensive notes on information presented in class and from reading assignments is active learning; critical thinking occurs when the student transforms these notes by (a) applying them to personal life experiences, (b) integrating them with previously learned concepts, (c) evaluating their validity, or (d) creating new ideas or possibilities with them.

- **Explicitly define critical thinking for students in terms of specific actions and attitudes that can be put into practice.** Although the call for critical thinking has been consistent since the early 1980s, there is much less consistency in how critical thinking has been defined or described. Following a 25-year review of the critical thinking literature, McMillan concluded that, "What is lacking in the research is a common definition of critical thinking and a clear definition of the nature of an experience that should enhance critical thinking" (1987, p. 37).

Our broad definition of critical thinking includes a wide variety of specific mental activities. The following list can be shared with students to help them understand what critical thinking actually is. Students can use this list to determine whether they are actually engaging in critical thinking:

- o Application: To apply theoretical principles or abstract concepts to practical, real-life situations and concrete problems (e.g., applying learned principles of critical thinking to class discussions and course exams).

- o Analysis: To break down (deconstruct) information into its parts in order to see the relationships among these parts, or the relationship between the parts and the whole (e.g., to identify the root causes of disagreements during class discussions; to distinguish relevant from irrelevant information; to identify and disclose hidden assumptions or biases).

- o Synthesis: To build up (reconstruct), combine, or integrate separate pieces of information to create a new pattern or alternative structure (e.g., to combine related ideas discussed in separate sections of the course to form a single, unified product, such as a written paper or concept map).

- o Evaluation: To judge the truth or value of ideas, data, or products (e.g., to judge the quality of a logical argument using established standards or learned criteria for critical thinking).

- o Deduction: To draw specific conclusions about particular examples which are logically consistent with, or necessarily follow from general principles and premises (e.g., to deduce what particular enforcement practices or disciplinary actions would follow if the college were to adopt a general "zero tolerance" drug policy on campus).

- o Induction: To draw out well-reasoned generalizations or principles from specific examples (e.g., to identify recurrent themes or categories among a variety of ideas generated during a group discussion).

- o Adduction: To make a case for an argument or position by accumulating supporting evidence in the form of logical arguments, factual information, or empirical research.

- o Refutation: To make a case against an argument or position by accumulating contradictory evidence in the form of logical arguments, factual information, or empirical research.

- o Extrapolation: To extend, expand, or project beyond information given and identify its implications for other areas (e.g., to extrapolate from present trends to construct an image of the future).

o Hypothetical Reasoning: To create tentative ideas or explanations for purposes of testing their validity or predicting their accuracy (e.g., to develop a survey or questionnaire designed to test the hypothesis that students are dissatisfied with the social climate on campus).

o Perspective-Taking: To view an issue from different viewpoints or positions in order to gain a more complete understanding (e.g., to view an issue from the perspective of someone different than yourself in terms of gender, age, or race).

o Divergent Thinking: Wide-focus thinking which serves to generate many different ideas (e.g., brainstorming multiple potential solutions to a problem).

o Convergent Thinking: Focused thinking which eliminates multiple ideas to decide on one particular option or alternative (e.g., to identify the best solution to a problem from a list of different solution strategies).

- **Discuss common critical-thinking errors based primarily on the work of Ruggiero (1996) and Wade & Tavris (1990):**

  o Over generalization: drawing general conclusions on the basis of an insufficient number of observations. (For example, concluding that a group of people are "all that way" or "most of them are that way" on the basis of just a few observations.)

  o Selective Perception: focusing only on information that supports your ideas and overlooking any information that contradicts them. (For example, a racially prejudiced person recalls particular examples to support his racial stereotype, but fails to consider instances which do not fit the stereotype.)

  o Using black-and-white/either-or reasoning. (For example, thinking that human behavior must be caused by either genetics or environment, but overlooking the fact that is often caused by a combination of these two factors.)

  o Assuming that two coincidental events must have a cause-effect relationship. (For example, crime rates increased during the same time period when parents report using less physical punishment with their children, therefore failure of parents to physically punish their children has caused an increase in the crime rate.)

  o Creating a straw man, i.e., attributing an idea to someone who never actually expressed that idea and then proceeding to attack it. (For instance, someone who claims to be "pro-choice" on the abortion issue is attacked for not being "pro-life.")

  o Appealing to authority or prestige rather than to reason. (For example, "Doctors prescribe this medicine, therefore it must be good for you.")

- Appealing to tradition rather than to reason. (For example, "This is the way it's always been done, so there's no reason why we should do it differently.")

- Appealing to popularity or the majority rather than to reason. (For example, "Everybody I know uses it, so it must be a good product.")

- Reaching conclusions on the basis of emotion rather than reason. (For example, "If I feel strongly about it, then it must be true.")

- Attacking the person, rather than the person's argument. (For example, "You're too young and inexperienced to know what you're talking about.")

- Assuming that critical thinking means being critical. (Critical thinking is not synonymous with negative thinking; it also involves thinking constructively, such as solving problems, thinking creatively, and coming up with new ideas and fresh approaches.)

- **Model or role-play the process of critical thinking for your students.**

  - Instead of immediately suggesting solutions for college adjustment challenges, first put yourself in the problem situation, as if you were a student, and think through the process of solving the problem out loud. This enables you to model critical thinking for your students and allows them to witness the process of problem solving in addition to its final product. You could even ask students to bring college-adjustment dilemmas to class for you to think through and attempt to resolve in front of them. A variation of this procedure would be for you to role-play a scene involving common critical-thinking errors, and then replay the scene with the characters displaying effective critical thinking skills.

- **Have students think aloud while they attempt to solve problems and resolve dilemmas.**

  - Research has shown that the quality of students' higher-level thinking is enhanced when they are asked to think out loud while they solve problems (Ahlum-Heather & DiVesta, 1986). Thinking aloud probably helps by causing students to consciously pay attention to their thinking and change these hidden thought processes into oral communication which can then be responded to and improved via feedback from others (Resnick, 1986).

- **After students have communicated their ideas, have them reflect on their thought processes to see whether they thought critically, and, if so, what form of critical thinking they used.**

  - Occasionally giving students some "pause time" in class lets them reflect on the quality of their thinking and decide whether they have used the thought processes and attitudes associated with critical thinking. For example, after a small-group or whole-class discussion, have students reflect on the quality of the thinking they displayed during the discussion and have them share these personal reflections verbally or in writing (for example, in the form of a short, post-discussion minute paper). Research has shown that high-achieving college students tend to reflect on their thought processes during learning and are aware of the cognitive strategies they use (Weinstein & Underwood, 1985). When such "meta-cognition" (thinking about thinking) and self-monitoring can be learned by students, the quality of their thinking skills is enhanced (Resnick, 1986).

- **Pose questions to students that provoke critical thinking.**

  o Alison King has conducted research that shows that students can learn to generate their own higher-level thinking questions. Using a technique that she calls "guided peer questioning," students are provided with a series of generic question stems that prompt different forms of critical thinking, such as:

    "What would happen if ___?"
    "What is the difference between ___ and ___?"
    "What are the implications of ___?"
    "Why is ___ important?"
    "What is another way to look at ___?" (King, 1995).

  Relative to a control group of students who simply partake in small-group discussion following a lecture presentation, students who are provided with high-level thinking questions beforehand have been found to: (a) ask a greater number of critical thinking questions and fewer rote recall questions in subsequent small-group interactions without being provided with question prompts, (b) elicit more high-level reasoning responses and elaborated explanations from teammates, and (c) exhibit greater academic achievement on test questions involving higher-level thinking (King, 1990).

- **Provide students with opportunities to practice critical thinking skills within the context of peer interaction.**

Research has consistently revealed that, when college students are required to engage in face-to-face discussion of course concepts with their peers, they are more likely to develop critical thinking skills than by merely listening to lectures and recording course notes. For example, Kulik and Kulik (1979) conducted a comprehensive review of research designed to assess the effectiveness of different college teaching strategies. They found that student discussion groups were significantly more effective for promoting students' problem-solving skills than the traditional lecture method.

Evidence for the value of having students explicitly practice critical thinking skills during peer interaction is again provided by Alison King. Her research involved a variation of the above procedure, which she calls "reciprocal peer questioning." In this procedure, students listen to a presentation and individually generate 2–3 relevant questions pertaining to the presentation, using question stems designed to elicit higher-level thinking responses which are provided to them by the instructor. Then students form two-member groups in which one member poses a question and the other member adopts the role of explainer/respondent; later, the students reverse roles.

Research on students who engage in this structured pair interaction reveals that they are more likely to display higher-level thinking in group discussions and on course examinations (King, 1995).

- **Create small groups of students (3–5) in which each member is assigned a specific critical-thinking role (e.g., analysis, synthesis, evaluation, application) with respect to the learning task.**

These roles can be depicted visually for students in the form of a graphic organizer, such as a content-by-process matrix, which juxtaposes key critical thinking processes with key course concepts. To ensure that students "stretch" their range of critical thinking skills, have students rotate critical thinking roles on successive small-group tasks.

The content-by process matrix provides students with a visible structure that helps them identify the type of cognitive processes they are expected to engage in when learning particular course content. The importance of providing such explicit structure for first-year students is underscored by Erickson and Strommer in *Teaching College Freshmen*:

> Structure is one source of support for freshmen, and we can provide it with explicit and clear instructions about what students are to do when they are "actively involved." The instructions not only call for an end product, but they also outline what students should consider along the way. Eventually, we hope students will learn to think through these situations without so many prompts. Initially, however, freshmen need them to guide thinking. (1991, p. 119)

- **Create cognitive dissonance or disequilibrium in the minds of students with respect to course concepts and issues.**

Research suggests that instructional practices that promote critical thinking are those that create cognitive dissonance or disequilibrium in students and prods them to consider different perspectives or multiple viewpoints (Brookfield, 1987; Kurfiss, 1988). The following practices are recommended as strategies for giving students that state of cognitive disequilibrium.

Select readings which present alternative viewpoints to those presented in the textbook. For example, have students compare certain information in the textbook with that from another source with a different perspective. This strategy should help combat the "dualistic" thinking of first-year students, which often leads them to believe that there are only right and wrong answers to problems or issues (Perry, 1970). Also, deliberately invite guest speakers to visit the class with differing perspectives on course topics. When deciding on the sequence of course topics or concepts, consider arranging their order in a way that juxtaposes and highlights incompatible viewpoints or perspectives.

Lee Shulman, president of the Carnegie Foundation for the Advancement of Teaching, is a strong advocate of this strategy. Here he describes how difficult it is to stimulate critical thinking monologically:

> I work very hard at trying to represent multiple perspectives. I try to build my course materials so that as soon as an idea has been offered persuasively, another idea that challenges it comes next. . . it's a dialectical view of what it means to teach something to somebody else, which is to force them to confront contradictions and counterpoints. (quoted in Miller, 1997, p. 5)

- **Incorporate comparison-and-contrast questions into lectures, tests, and assignments.**

During class discussions, raise questions that call for multiple student perspectives. (For example, "Who doesn't agree with what's being said?" "Would someone else like to express an opposing viewpoint?") Try the following strategies to engage your students in critically thinking about viewpoints different from their own:

- o Assign a one-minute paper or reaction paper at the end of class that asks students if there was any point made or position taken during the day's session that they strongly question or challenge, and then use their responses as springboards for discussion in the next class session.

- o Use student-centered instructional methods which take you "off stage," exposing students to the perspectives of other students and reducing their perception of you as the absolute authority. For example, have students who hold diverse viewpoints on a certain issue join together to form (a) small discussion groups, (b) student debate teams, or (c) panel discussions.

- o Play the role of "devil's advocate," using the Socratic method to prod students to see the pros and cons of their position on an issue. For example, persuade students to buy into a certain position, then proceed to expose its flaws.

- o Have students engage in "reverse thinking" by requiring them to switch their original position on an issue being discussed in class. This can serve to combat "either-or"/"black-and-white" thinking and help students adopt a more balanced position on controversial issues.

- o Have students research and prepare to defend both sides of an issue, then randomly assign them to argue for one of the positions in class or on an exam. For instance, two students might be given the assignment of researching both sides of a college-life issue, such as whether the legal age for use of alcohol should be lowered or remain the same. Before the debate begins, a flip of the coin could determine which side of the issue each student will take. As Bergquist and Phillips point out, this type of activity encourages students to "appreciate the complexity of intellectual issues and the inherent danger of simplistic thinking" (1981, p. 116).

o   Have students role-play with someone with whom they disagree strongly.

D. Suggested Outline for Addressing Topics in Chapter 5

STEP I: BEGIN WITH A LECTURE LAUNCHER OR ICEBREAKER ACTIVITY
STEP II: EMPLOY A VARIETY OF CLASSROOM ACTIVITIES
    a.   Use the PowerPoint presentation from *Multimedia Manager 2007* resource
    b.   Expand on key lesson themes
    c.   Involve peer leaders
    d.   Use chapter exercises
    e.   Engage students in learning through case studies
STEP III: REVIEW & PREVIEW
    a.   Address common questions and concerns about the topic
    b.   Writing reflection
    c.   Prepare for next class

Expanded Lesson Plan

STEP I: Lecture Launchers and Icebreakers

- Ask students how much their classes require or encourage them to develop the four aspects of critical thinking skills. Explain to them that the answer will vary with the teaching styles of their instructors and with how much preparation they bring to class. It may also vary according to the size and format of the class. Tell them that even in a lecture with many students, a talented teacher can stimulate their ability to form abstractions, think creatively, think systematically, and communicate well.

- If you have the ability to project the Internet in your classroom, consider using the practice of evaluating web pages to illustrate the process of critical thinking. A controversial issue – say, creationism versus evolution – will yield several pages that present each side as the only "truth." Another site you could use is Martin Luther King, Jr.: A True Historical Examination (http://www.martinlutherking.org/). At first glance, it looks like a scholarly study of the work of the civil rights leader. A deeper reading, however, reveals its strong biases. Ask your students which critical thinking skills they used to deduce whether or not a site is an objective, valid source. You may also get into a discussion about the ethics of presentation (i.e., is it fair for a site to present itself as a scholarly work, when it's really propaganda?).

STEP II: Classroom Activities

a. Use the PowerPoint presentations in *Multimedia Manager 2007* resource to complement your mini lecture.

b. Key Lesson Themes

- Choose from the ideas listed in the margins of your text: p. 81 (College Helps You Develop Critical Thinking Skills), p. 83 (Going From Certainty to Healthy Uncertainty), p. 84 (A Higher-Order Thinking Process and Collaboration Fosters Critical Thinking), p. 85 (A Skill to Carry You Through Life), etc. to engage students in problem-based or issue-centered tasks to stimulate critical thinking. The critical thinking literature strongly suggests that these active-learning tasks be centered on (a) problems that may not be readily solved, (b) issues to be discussed or debated, or (c) decision-making tasks that require exploration of equally appealing alternatives.

c. Group Activities

- Do the following exercise to examine the four aspects of critical thinking through practical application:

  1. Form groups of four students. Each student in each group should be placed in charge of one of the four critical thinking stages. They will record a list of examples of their particular stage, based on the classroom experiences of all four students, adding how each particular experience helps make learning more meaningful for them.

  2. Issue the following instructions to each group: Consider several courses you are taking now. In a group, discuss the following issues. Compare your classroom experiences with different instructors in terms of:

     o **Forming Abstractions** - Do they expect or encourage students to raise questions? Do they present evidence and challenge you to interpret it? Do they challenge class members to restate or paraphrase the main idea of a lecture?
     o **Creative Thinking** – Do they help you practice looking at several sides of an issue? Do they ask for your ideas on an issue? Do they ask you to keep an open mind on a question that you at first think has an obvious right answer? Do they use brainstorming strategies in which ideas can be generated without being prejudged?
     o **Systematic Thinking** – Do they give you practice in following a careful line of reasoning? Do they ask you to fill in the missing steps

in an argument? Do they ask you to judge whether an idea is adequately supported by logic or data?

  o **Communication** – Do they have a process for encouraging students to speak—even shy students? Do they ask a member of the class to clarify a point for the benefit of other students? Have you volunteered an idea? Have you made an effort to keep an open mind about something about which you already had a strong opinion? Have you participated in a group or classroom brainstorming effort? Have you talked with the instructor before or after class or during office hours? Have you discussed ideas from the course or asked questions of other students in the class?

3. Bring groups together after 20 minutes and put the final lists on the board. Ask how such experiences facilitated their learning.

d. Peer Leader Assistance

- Use the following exercise to find links between students' learning style preferences and their critical thinking skills; to apply the critical thinking process to a topic about which students have strong feelings; and to overcome the tendency to use emotional arguments without first applying reason

  1. This exercise attempts to answer the question, "Can your learning preferences (see Chapter 3) affect the ease or difficulty with which you complete the four stages of critical thinking?" It may be easier for intuitive (N) learners to find abstractions amid details and brain storm possibilities (Steps 1 and 2), whereas sensing (S) learners may do well in Step 3 where they can list ideas into some logical order. Thinking (T) learners may also find Step 3 comes naturally to them, whereas feeling (F) learners may complete Step 3 by prioritizing their values, rather than be the logic of the situation. Present your students with the following scenario:

     To cut costs and accommodate students who wish to complete their education faster, the administration is considering dividing the year into four equal terms of thirteen weeks each. One term would run January through March, a second term would run April through June, a third July through September, and a fourth October through December. Any holidays-such as Christmas and Thanksgiving-would be shortened to no more than two days to accommodate the schedule. Faculty would teach only three terms a year, on a rotating basis, meaning that some courses might not be available year round. Although most students would attend classes only three out of four terms, students would have the option of graduating early if they attended all four terms. Due to a slightly shorter schedule, class length would increase by roughly ten minutes a period. The average student course load would be four courses per term. The highly popular president of your student government, who is in favor of the proposal, has asked you to take a stand on this issue at a campus-wide meeting.

2. Divide your students into groups of four or five (preferably by opposite N/S and T/F preferences).

3. Ask them to list the broad abstract ideas inherent in this proposal to change the school term. What are the truths or arguments here? What are the key ideas? What larger concepts do the details suggest? What is the administration really trying to accomplish?

4. Next, ask them to brainstorm some new possibilities. What questions do the large ideas suggest? What new questions can be asked about the value of adjusting the schedule? What other possibilities might there be besides dividing the year into four equal parts? What are some possible effects of such a change on students? On faculty? Avoid making immediate decisions. Put off closure. Reject nothing at first.

5. Finally, have them organize new ideas and possibilities in a logical order. In what direction do the facts really point? What are the best solutions? To leave the schedule alone? To offer options? Is there some important additional information that needs to be gathered and evaluated before it is possible to reach a conclusion? Ultimately, what new abstractions and new conclusions have resulted from the group's thinking?

6. For the final step, have your students use the results of the group thinking process to write a paper that precisely communicates their ideas to others. Are their conclusions well supported? Make certain their conclusions take all parties (the majority of students, faculty, and others) into account. At the end of the paper, ask them to state whether they believe their learning style made any of these steps easy or difficult to follow and why.

e. Case Studies

Michel
Michel crashed through the doorway of his residence hall room and slammed the door. "I hate women!" he yelled to his roommate, Karl. Karl asked him what was wrong. Michel sneered. "I just don't understand them. Women. Toni just broke our date for Friday night just because she found out I was drunk out of my mind at the ball game. Don't I have a right to have fun sometimes? And why should what I do when I'm out with the boys have anything to do with what goes on between Toni and me?" Karl opened his mouth to say something but Michel raised his right hand. "Shut it, Karl. Nothing you say is gonna change my mind about this."

Discussion Questions:

1. How is Michel responding? What is the basis for his arguments?
2. What kind of critical thinking errors is Michel making?
3. What are the implications of what Karl might say?
4. What is another way to look at Michel's situation?

Susannah

Susannah has to write an argument essay for her freshman composition class. She chooses underage drinking as her topic. Initially, Susannah plans to argue that the drinking age should be raised to 25. In high school, Susannah's friend Tia was killed when an 18-year-old drunk driver flipped his car and sent Tia's over a guardrail. But as Susannah researches her topic, she finds information about alcohol abuse and incidents of drunk driving in other countries where the drinking age is even lower than it is in the United States. She starts to wonder if it is Americans' attitudes toward alcohol that is the problem, and not the drinking age itself. Writing the paper becomes frustrating, as Susannah no longer knows what thesis she is trying to prove.

Discussion Questions:
1. Which general thinking skills is Susannah employing in her research?
2. Which skills could she try to clarify her stance on the issue?
3. What kind of thesis statement could Susannah write that would incorporate both sides of the issue, and yet still make a strong argument for or against something?

f. Chapter Exercises

- **Exercise 5.1: Reflecting on Arguments**
  Because this exercise takes over a week to complete, have students do the exercise then discuss the results in class.

- **Exercise 5.2: Learning about a Liberal Education**
  If you require students to interview their academic advisor, this assignment can be included with that interview.

- **Exercise 5.3: The Challenge of Classroom Thinking**
  This exercise can be done during class and discussed in small groups.

- **Exercise 5.4: Hard or Easy**
  This exercise can also be done during class and discussed in small groups.

- **Exercise 5.5: Handling It Emotionally or Logically**
  Assign this exercise to small groups (2 to 4 students) and have them completed in class. You may also consider having each group perform their scripts; if so, try to assign each group a different scenario (inventing as many extras as you need).

REVIEW

a. Address Common Questions and Concerns of First-Year Students:

- *The professor says this might be right or that might be right. Why doesn't he just tell us which one?*
  Answer: Many professors are more concerned about how students arrive at an answer rather than if it is right or not. Explain and demonstrate to students that there are times when there is more than one correct answer.

- *I came to college to learn from the experts. Why do I have to listen to other students discuss a topic in class? It's such a waste of my time!*
  Answer: Participating in class discussion is a good way to gather information and listen to others' opinions. Help students realize that class discussions are a good way to develop critical thinking and active learning skills.

- *I don't see why I have to check so many sources in order to write a paper on one topic. Isn't one person's opinion enough?*
  Answer: Students need to learn that checking sources helps them to develop not only critical thinking skills, but research skills too. There is often more than one theory or opinion about a topic. It is also a good way for students to learn about a topic as a "whole." Explain to students that this gives them a chance to gather evidence and consider alternatives.

- *Why do I have to explain why I think something is right? Isn't just saying it's right enough?*
  Answer: Explaining information and supporting evidence is a must for students to learn. This skill is not only important in college, but will prove to be an important life tool. Class is a good time to practice how to precisely communicate your ideas to others. Whether in school, at work, or home, they will be asked to do this over and over again.

b. Writing Reflection

- **Exercise 5.4: Hard or Easy?**
  Consider assigning this exercise as a short writing project to be completed out of class or as a journal entry.

PREVIEW FOR NEXT CLASS

E. Test Questions

Multiple Choice - choose ONE answer per question.

1. Which one of the following aspects of critical thinking involves discussing logical ideas and general principles?
   a. Systematic thinking
   b. Evaluation
   c. Precise communication
   d. Abstract thinking

2. Which one of the following statements is NOT good advice for developing effective thinking and writing habits?
   a. Be willing to say, "I don't know."
   b. Get used to clarifying what you mean and asking others to do so.
   c. Try to adopt the attitude that you must win every argument.
   d. Judge an argument on its merits, rather than on the basis of who said it.

3. A critical thinker possesses all of the following EXCEPT
   a. the ability to analyze a problem.
   b. the ability to imagine solutions, weight them by rational criteria, and commit to one.
   c. the ability to create a simplistic analysis of a compounded issue.
   d. a tolerance for ambiguity and complexity.

4. In college, the term "argument" refers to
   a. a physical confrontation.
   b. an emotional confrontation.
   c. a formal complaint you file against your professor.
   d. a collection of reasons and information that form logical support of some idea.

5. Which of the following is NOT a question a good critical thinker would ask?
   a. Why does Speaker X feel so strongly about the issue?
   b. Did Speaker X move me to feeling strongly about the issue?
   c. Has Speaker X adequately supported his viewpoint?
   d. What was Speaker X trying to say?

6. Chances are when you land a job, your employer is going to be more interested in how well you _____ than in how well you can memorize information.
   a. dress
   b. budget
   c. write
   d. think

7. In a liberal education, students are taught to investigate
   a. all sides of a question.
   b. all possible solutions to a problem.
   c. a and b
   d. none of the above

8. The most creative idea starts with two stages; brainstorming and
   a. blending.
   b. decision making.
   c. refinement.
   d. none of the above

9. Which of the following statements will NOT help you to think critically?
   a. Attack the argument, not the person.
   b. Don't beg.
   c. Appeal to authority.
   d. Avoid hasty generalizations.

10. When evaluating information on the Internet, ask yourself the following:
    a. Is it credible?
    b. Who is the author?
    c. Does it reflect mainstream opinions?
    d. all of the above

True/False

11. A strong argument appeals to your emotions the most.

12. If you read two opposing views about the same topic, you must determine that one of them is wrong.

13. Creative thinking refers to seeking connections, finding new possibilities, and rejecting nothing.

14. Employers are more interested in how well you can think than in how well you can memorize information.

15. Your high school English teacher gave you firm rules for writing, yet your college English teacher has her own set of rules. One of them must be wrong.

Short Answer

16. Name the four aspects of critical thinking.

17. Name three components of a strong argument.

18. Give an example of passive learning and then illustrate how it can be converted to an active learning process by utilizing critical thinking skills.

19. Explain the differences between brainstorming and refinement.

20. List and explain the steps of the process for generating ideas.

Essay

21. Think about the courses you are taking this term and illustrate how each one encourages each of the four aspects of critical thinking.

22. Explore the process of creative thinking. Begin by describing what defines creative thinking. Then, choose an idea and demonstrate your creative thoughts about it.

23. Explore why critical thinking is at the core of a liberal education.

24. Identify a newsworthy item that is clearly polarizing the population. Defend both positions.

25. Using the nine C's for evaluating Internet resources, critique an Internet article to be distributed by your instructor.

CHAPTER 5 ANSWER KEY
1. d, p. 87
2. c, pp. 86-87
3. c, p. 84
4. d, p. 85
5. b, p. 86
6. d, p. 82
7. c, p. 87
8. c, p. 88
9. c, p. 90
10. d, p. 93
11. false, p. 87
12. false, pp. 88-89
13. true, p. 88
14. true, p. 83
15. false, pp. 84-85
16. Abstract thinking, creative thinking, systematic thinking, and precise communication, pp. 88
17. Answers will vary, pp. 86-87
18. Answers will vary, pp.82-83

F. Web Resources

Critical Thinking Guidelines – http://www.coun.uvic.ca/learn/crit.html
The University of Victoria hosts this site, which lists some general guidelines for thinking critically.

Education Is Not Found in a Book – http://www.higher-ed.org/AEQ/if-ju.htm
Introduce this essay, written by a student at the University of South Carolina, to your class. It talks about how college provides opportunities to develop critical thinking skills – and how these opportunities mean very little if students aren't willing to put in the work.

Tutorial in Critical Reasoning – http://commhum.mccneb.edu/argument/summary.htm
This interactive tutorial will help students identify the argument of an essay, as well as recognize structure, and search for conclusions. Additional writing exercises are included on the site.

Intro to Creative Thinking – http://www.virtualsalt.com/crebook1.htm
Take a look at this extensive article, written by Robert Harris, author of *Creative Problem Solving: A Step-by-Step Approach*. It covers everything from myths about creative thinking to positive attitudes for creativity.

Thinking Critically about the Web – http://www.library.ucla.edu/libraries/college/help/critical/
Since the Internet is often the first place students turn for a source-based paper, it's crucial that they learn how to apply their critical thinking skills to evaluating the value and reliability of web pages. Try to work at least one Internet-based exercise into your lesson plan while teaching this chapter.

Collaborative Learning – http://scholar.lib.vt.edu/ejournals/JTE/jte-v7n1/gokhale.jte-v7n1.html
This study, originally published in the Journal of Technology Education, focuses on how collaborative learning enhances critical thinking—A fascinating read.

Evaluating Website Content - www.iss.stthomas.edu/webtruth/evaluate.htm

Integrating Critical Thinking Skills into the Classroom -
http://www.kcmetro.cc.mo.us/longview/ctac/index.htm,
http://www.uky.edu/LCC/PHI/critthnk.html

Decision Making Skills - http://www.hooah4health.com/spirit/decisions.htm

G. For More Information

Bartholomew, Robert E. and Benjamin Radford. (2003). *Hoaxes, myths, and mania: Why we need critical thinking*. New York: Prometheus Books.

DiSpezio, Michael A. (1997). *Great critical thinking puzzles*. New York: Sterling Publishing.

Glasser, Edward M. (1941). *An experiment in the development of critical thinking*. New York: AMS Press.

Toulmin, Stephen E. (1958). *The uses of argument*. New York: Cambridge University Press.

Walter, Timothy L. (2003). *Critical thinking: Building the basics (2nd ed)*. San Francisco: Wadsworth Publishing.

Chapter 6: Listening, Note Taking, and Participating

By Jeanne L. Higbee, Professor and Faculty Chair, Center for Research on Developmental Education and Urban Literacy, General College, University of Minnesota

Ideas for Instruction and Instructor Training	Videos and CD-ROMs	Media Resources for Instructors	Media Resources for Students
Instructor's Manual (IM) Includes a brief lesson plan for Chapter 6, chapter objectives, lecture launchers, commentary on exercises in the book, and case studies. **Test Bank (in IM)** Multiple Choice, True/False, Short Answer and Essay Questions. Also available in ExamView® electronic format, which can be customized to fit your needs.	***10 Things Every Student Needs to Know to Study Video*** 6-minute segment entitled "Taking Notes." **ExamView® CD-ROM** Computerized version of the Test Bank items for Chapter 6.	**JOININ™** Hand-held audience response device allows students immediate response to multiple-choice questions, polls, and interactive exercises. **Multimedia Manager 2007 CD-ROM** PowerPoint presentations, video clips, images, and web links help with assembly, editing, and presentation of multimedia lectures.	**iLrn® Pin-Coded Website** Contains self-assessments, electronic journals that encourage students to reflect on their progress, essay questions and exercises, and Test Your Knowledge interactive quizzes for Chapter 6. **InfoTrac® College Edition** May be bundled with text. *Keywords:* college success, liberal arts, goal setting, values, colleges, universities. **WebTutor™ Toolbox** Online course management tool for WebCT™ or Blackboard preloaded with text-specific content and media resources for Chapter 6.

A. Chapter Objectives

1. To assist students in learning how to master information presented in a lecture
2. To convince students to adopt an efficient note taking system
3. To demonstrate that an efficient note taking system is also a powerful study aid when preparing for exams
4. To show students how the five senses can assist in learning and remembering
5. To encourage students to participate in class discussions

B. Timing of Chapter Coverage

You may find that this chapter is best taught after Chapter 3, "Learning Styles." In many courses, students begin falling behind the very first day of class if they do not have an efficient method of taking lecture notes. The information in this chapter will provide students with strategies for not only getting involved in class, but also with ways to gather important classroom information. First-year students need to learn how to "cope" in the classroom environment and adapt to lectures as quickly as possible. This chapter's information can help them do just that.

C. About This Chapter

Students are likely to comment that in contrast to many high school classes, which are focused on a textbook, many college classes are focused on the lectures and the textbook may be supportive rather than primary. Because of this essential difference, college students must listen attentively to lectures and write down both main ideas and supporting details in ways that are clear, comprehensive, and conducive to learning and recall later on. If they do not listen and take effective notes, there may not be a textbook to fall back on like there was in high school.

As a rule, testing is fairly frequent in high school. It is usually much less frequent in college. In fact, at some schools, instructors of first-year courses test only twice during the term and once during finals. Consequently, there are long periods of time between the delivery of the information and the demonstration of knowledge. This suggests, once again, the importance of accurate and effective note taking.

After discussing these essential differences, you might want to shift the focus to memory. As the text points out, most forgetting occurs within 24 hours of learning. What is significant about this is that it suggests a coping strategy: students need to take advantage of the 24-hour period within which learning occurs.

Having a note taking system is paramount to a student's success in the classroom. With the chapter information and exercises, help them to identify a system that will complement their learning styles. The Cornell Method is a proven way for most students to take notes. However, allow them to be creative.

This chapter gives specific strategies for before, during, and after class as well as class participation. Make sure students know these strategies and can determine how they will improve their classroom experience and overall learning.

D. Suggested Outline for Addressing Topics in Chapter 6

STEP I: BEGIN WITH A LECTURE LAUNCHER OR ICEBREAKER ACTIVITY
STEP II: EMPLOY A VARIETY OF CLASSROOM ACTIVITIES
    a. Use the PowerPoint presentation from *Multimedia Manager 2007* resource
    b. Expand on key lesson themes
    c. Involve peer leaders
    d. Use chapter exercises
    e. Engage students in learning through case studies
STEP III: REVIEW & PREVIEW
    a. Address common questions and concerns about the topic
    b. Writing reflection
    c. Prepare for next class

Expanded Lesson Plan

STEP I: Lecture Launchers and Icebreakers

- You may want to begin by asking students to discuss how college classes are structured differently from high school classes and how they are adjusting to this transition. Examining these differences may help them to bridge the gaps they are experiencing as new students. Ask them to consider and discuss some of the following questions:

  - How are they adjusting to the transition in the classroom?
  - Are some college classes easier to take notes in? Why?
  - What does the instructor do to facilitate students' understanding of lectures?
  - What does the instructor do to make it easy to take notes?
  - What strategies can make note taking easier?

- Ask students to share with their partners any difficulties they are experiencing with lectures. From there, you can begin to discuss student experiences in the classroom with lectures, note taking, and participation. This will give you a place to start as well as evaluate your students' skill levels.

- One way to introduce the use of senses in the learning process is to get your students thinking about their own sensory preferences. You can access the site for VARK online. The free, printable learning style inventory consists of 13 questions and can be downloaded from http://www.vark-learn.com/english/index.asp and distributed to your students. It measures a person's preference for four kinds of learning: Visual, Aural, "Read/Write," and Kinesthetic. You can use the VARK assessment to introduce your students to the concept of sensory-aided memory before launching into a discussion of the six senses discussed in the text.

STEP II: Classroom Activities

a. Use the PowerPoint presentations in *Multimedia Manager 2007* resource to complement your mini lecture.

b. Key Lesson Themes

- **Testing Memory:**

  1. Ask your students to think back to a lecture they heard in another class the day before.
  2. Have them jot down as many main ideas and supporting details as they can remember.
  3. As part of a homework assignment or in class, have them compare these lists to the notes they took in that class.
  4. Students quickly realize how incomplete their lists are. This activity demonstrates, more clearly than any lecture could, how important it is to review.

Effective Note-Taking:

1. Ask your students to take notes on this lecture. Afterward, give them an additional 10 minutes to fill in the recall column.
2. Next, have students pair up to compare the most important ideas presented in the lecture. Have them discuss whether reading the assignment prior to the lecture informed their note taking abilities.
3. An alternative is to instruct your students not to take notes on the lecture. Then deliver another mini lecture of equal difficulty, but this time, instruct the students to take notes. During your next class meeting, quiz them on both lectures to demonstrate that their recall of the second lecture was greater.

c. Group Activities

- Ask students to try and determine which of their senses they use most when trying to sort and remember material for class. You might have them form groups by preferred senses. If some individuals are standing alone, put them in another group and have them explain their method and listen to others explain theirs. **See Exercise 6.1**

d. Peer Leader Assistance

- Ask students to take out the notebook they use for this or any other class. Pair them up and have them show one page of their notes to their partner. Let each partner see if they can "make sense" of this page of notes. They can give feedback on the following:

  - Can they understand the general idea of the notes?
  - Can they identify the topic of the lecture?
  - How do the notes look to them?

Show the students a sample of how you take notes and discuss with the students the strengths and weakness of your note taking style.

e. Case Studies

Nate

Nate is a first-year student. He has had difficulty concentrating during the first week of lectures in his economics class and already seems to be losing his focus in his other classes. Listening to lectures and taking notes is extremely difficult for him. He's finding that his notes do not make sense and he seems to be lacking important lecture information. At the end of the first week, he goes to his economics professor's office hours. He then proceeds to tell the professor that when he was in elementary school he was diagnosed with Attention Deficit Hyperactivity Disorder (ADHF). He confides that he has been taking medication and getting some additional assistance from teachers with note taking and studying for tests, beginning in elementary school and right up through high school.

Discussion Questions:
1. What suggestions would you make to help Nate?
2. What strategies do you have that might help Nate in other classes?
3. What ways could instructors adjust their teaching style to assist students like Nate?
4. What other ways could the instructor help Nate?

Rita

Rita has recently returned to college and started taking night classes. After high school, she started working full time in a law firm to make money, gain experience, and see if she would be interested in pursuing law school. She works full time during the day, and lives at home with her parents. Rita's night classes are long and she is usually very tired from her workday when she gets there. All Rita can seem to do is sit back in her lectures and take notes. She feels too tired to ask questions and participate in class activities. She knows that class participation counts for 20% of her grade in one class. Rita knows she can pass the class with at least a C by doing this, but it is not her best effort. She is trying to get good grades now so when she applies to law school, she will have a competitive GPA. Rita wants to get "A"s in her classes.

Discussion Questions:
1. What are Rita's issues in this situation?
2. What strategies would you suggest Rita use in the classroom?
3. What strategies outside the classroom would you suggest for Rita?
4. How can Rita motivate herself to participate in class and in her learning?
5. How can Rita become a more active learner?

f. Chapter Exercises

- **Exercise 6.2: Comparing Notes**
  Give students a few minutes at the end of one of your lectures to do this exercise with a partner. (Or, you can use this as a Lecture Launcher). They will benefit from their partner's feedback. Have them identify the changes they want to make.

- **Exercise 6.3: Memory: Using a Recall Column**
  Working with partners or writing their findings on this exercise will be effective practice for students. With partners, have them test each other using the recall column and then discuss the exercise questions. Encourage students to begin to formulate a note taking system if they don't already have one.

STEP III: Review and Preview

REVIEW

a. Address Common Questions and Concerns of First-Year Students:

- *Why do I need to take notes? I can just read the text.*
  Answer: Just reading the text is not enough to effectively learn class material. Many times instructors present lecture material that supplements the textbook. Students need to realize that they may miss important information if they do not take notes.

- *Why do I have to take notes? I like to sit back and enjoy the lecture, and taking notes gets in the way.* Answer: Effective learning takes place when students are actively engaged with the lecture material. Explain to them some of the differences between active and passive students in the classroom (if you have not yet covered Chapter 4, "Engagement with Learning"). Remind them that note taking enhances active listening, furthers their absorption of the material, and provides additional structure to test preparation.

- *Why can't I just bring in a tape recorder?*
  Answer: While recording a lecture may be helpful in some ways, it may not be as effective as the student anticipates. Tell students that recording a lecture often insures that they will sit through it at least twice. This can be extremely time consuming. Encourage students to find other ways to get lecture information. However, if there's a reason students need to tape the lecture, commuters for example, may want to take advantage of listening to the taped lectures during their commute – remind them to ask their instructor's permission before doing so.

- *How can I take notes when he/she talks too fast?*
  Answer: Students sometimes run into this problem. First, remind them that they do not have to write down everything a professor says. Encourage them to explore other methods of filling in their notes, such as meeting with the professor or forming a study group to compare notes.

- *Should I take notes during a discussion?*
  Answer: Discussions are a part of active learning. Encourage students to write down key points and discussions. They may need to correlate discussion notes with their lecture notes, as well as determine their importance to the class material. Remind students that they may be responsible for the information presented during a discussion session on a later test.

- *If an outline is presented, should I copy it all down at the beginning of the lecture?*
  Answer: Encourage students to copy an outline as it's presented so they don't miss important lecture information.

b. Writing Reflection

- Give students a few minutes to answer the questions on page 126.

PREVIEW FOR NEXT CLASS

E. Test Questions

Multiple Choice - choose ONE answer per question.

1. Most forgetting takes place within _____ hour(s) of seeing or hearing something.
   a. 1
   b. 24
   c. 48
   d. 72

2. A(n) _____ learner might benefit from discussing coursework with friends.
   a. aural
   b. visual
   c. tactile
   d. interactive

3. A(n) _____ learner might benefit from typing lecture notes.
   a. aural
   b. visual
   c. tactile
   d. interactive

4. During lecture, you should focus on all of the following EXCEPT
   a. facts and figures.
   b. main concepts.
   c. central ideas.
   d. new information.

5. Which of the following is most important when it comes to effective note taking?
   a. Taping the lecture
   b. Memorizing the recall column
   c. Identifying the main points
   d. Writing the information down verbatim

6. According to the text, a student needs to master the following two skills to earn high grades:
   a. facts and figures.
   b. listening and note-taking.
   c. central ideas and new information.
   d. none of the above

7. Listening in class is like
   a. listening to a TV program.
   b. listening to a friend.
   c. listening to a speaker at a meeting.
   d. none of the above

8. One method for organizing notes is called
    a. Cornell format.
    b. Jewler method.
    c. College success method.
    d. none of the above

9. When using technology to take notes, remember that
    a. laptops are often poor tools for taking notes during class.
    b. computers are conducive to making marginal notes.
    c. laptops are conducive to circling important items.
    d. none of the above

10. To really learn, you must
    a. talk about what you're learning.
    b. write about what you're learning.
    c. relate what you're learning to past experiences.
    d. all of the above

True/False

11. During lecture, it is best to use shorthand and write down everything the teacher says verbatim.

12. It is not necessary or important to take notes on class discussion.

12. You cannot assume that college instructors lecture on the same material covered in the course text.

14. It is not a good idea to compare notes with another student.

15. A laptop computer is an excellent tool for taking notes in class.

Short Answer

16. In the Cornell format of note taking, the left margin on the paper is called the _____ _____.

17. After class, the 3Rs are _____, _____, and _____.

18. Name some methods of note taking other than outlining.

19. List some reasons why sharing notes can be a good practice.

20. List some reasons why sharing notes can be counterproductive.

Essay

21. Describe three strategies you can use to listen critically during a lecture. Explain the benefits of using them and why they will work.

22. Draw a diagram of the Cornell method of note taking and list the parts. Then, discuss the benefits of using a note taking system.

23. Describe some things you can do prior to the start of a lecture to prepare for learning and remembering.

24. Give a brief description of the note taking formats that the text recommends. Discuss your personal preference.

25. Describe the steps to follow when taking notes. Which one(s) do you need to work on the most and why?

CHAPTER 6 ANSWER KEY

1. b, p. 106
2. d, p. 107
3. c, p. 107
4. a, p. 109
5. c, p. 114
6. b, p. 104
7. d, p.109
8. a, p. 111
9. a, p. 119
10. d, p. 121
11. false, pp. 112, 122
12. false, p. 112
13. true, p. 119
14. false, p. 120
15. false, p. 119
16. recall column, p. 111
17. Respond, Recite, Review, pp. 119

F. Web Resources

Why We Forget – http://sarc.sdes.ucf.edu/learningskills/WhyWeForgetTEXT.html
The University of Central Florida hosts this web page, which lists seven common reasons for forgetting information, as well as suggestions to overcome each one.

Cornell System - http://www.ucc.vt.edu/stdysk/cornell.html

Note-Taking - http://www.dartmouth.edu/~acskills/success/notes.html
This page also includes tips on recognizing important information, as well as additional note-taking aids.

Listening Skills - http://www.infoplease.com/homework/listeningskills1.html

Participating in Class – http://www.drlynnfriedman.com/classparticipation.html
Clinical psychology Dr. Lynn Friedman offers her opinions as to why it's important to participate in class discussion, as well as suggestions on how to prepare to participate.

Applied Research – http://courseweb.gse.upenn.edu/~abrahaml/methods/appliedresearch.htm
A University of Pennsylvania master's degree candidate conducted applied research on "How Can I Create a Space for Less Vocal Students to Participate in Science Class?" The above link takes you to the index for the site, which goes through the methodology behind the project, as well as the results.

G. For More Information

DePorter, Bobbi and Mike Hernacki. (2000). *Quantum notes: Whole brain approaches to note-taking.* Oceanside, CA: Learning Forum.

Helgesen, Marc et al. (1995). *Active listening: Introducing skills for understanding (student's book 1).* New York: Cambridge University Press.

Kesselman-Turkel, Judi and Franklynn Peterson. (2003). *Note-taking made easy.* Madison, WI: University of Wisconsin Press.

Stanley, Christine A. (2002). *Engaging large classes: Strategies and techniques for college faculty.* Bolton, MA: Anker Pub Co.

Winter, Arthur and Ruth Winter. (1997). *Brain workout: Easy ways to power up your memory, sensory perception, and intelligence.* New York: St. Martin's Press.

Chapter 7: Reading Strategies

By Jeanne L. Higbee, Professor and Faculty Chair, Center for Research on Developmental Education and Urban Literacy, General College, University of Minnesota

Ideas for Instruction and Instructor Training	VIDEOS AND CD-ROMS	Media Resources for Instructors	Media Resources for Students
Instructor's Manual (IM) Includes a brief lesson plan for Chapter 7, chapter objectives, lecture launchers, commentary on exercises in the book, and case studies. **Test Bank (in IM)** Multiple Choice, True/False, Short Answer and Essay Questions. Also available in ExamView® electronic format, which can be customized to fit your needs.	***10 Things Every Student Needs to Know to Study Video*** 6-minute segment entitled "Improving Your Reading." **ExamView® CD-ROM** Computerized version of the Test Bank items for Chapter 7.	**JOININ™** Hand-held audience response device allows students immediate response to multiple-choice questions, polls, and interactive exercises. **Multimedia Manager 2007 CD-ROM** PowerPoint presentations, video clips, images, and web links help with assembly, editing, and presentation of multimedia lectures.	**iLrn® Pin-Coded Website** Contains self-assessments, electronic journals that encourage students to reflect on their progress, essay questions and exercises, and Test Your Knowledge interactive quizzes for Chapter 7. **InfoTrac® College Edition** May be bundled with text. *Keywords:* college success, liberal arts, goal setting, values, colleges, universities. **WebTutor™ Toolbox** Online course management tool for WebCT™ or Blackboard preloaded with text-specific content and media resources for Chapter 7.

A. Chapter Objectives

1. To distinguish between reading a textbook and reading for pleasure
2. To encourage the continuation or adoption of systematic approaches to reading textbooks
3. To facilitate vocabulary development
4. To establish reading techniques as part of overall study strategies
5. To learn how to monitor reading comprehension
6. To strengthen critical reading

B. Timing of Chapter Coverage

Students will be given reading assignments during the first week of class. Many of these assignments will involve textbook reading because many of their first-term classes will be introductory (survey) courses. Your students may start to become inundated with the amount of textbook reading that is expected of them. It is particularly important that this chapter is covered in time to allow students to begin learning the required textbook material so they can adequately prepare for their first college exams.

C. About This Chapter

One of the most difficult aspects of the transition from learning in high school to mastering course work in college is developing strategies for reading different types of textbooks. In the beginning, first-year students tend to allocate too little time to adequately comprehend and retain textbook material. They may also be overly dependent on highlighting or underlining without understanding the role of other strategies that are used when reviewing for exams. Whatever method students choose, they should keep in mind that their ultimate purpose is to be able to read actively and critically, determining what is important, and creating a system for review. If this is done successfully, there should be no need for students to reread entire chapters of the text prior to exams.

Since reading in college is more challenging to students, help them focus on the strategies in this chapter that will improve their reading skills. Explain to students that they will need to know that the amount and type of reading may change from what they have been used to and they will also have to change their approach to textbook reading. For example, a textbook may be used as the main body of information in a course that will be included on exams. Let's face it, students will have to be able to actively read and learn this material if they are going to be successful.

This chapter offers solid strategies for working with textbook material. Encourage the development of a reading strategy and the use of the many skills included in the text such as mapping, monitoring comprehension, awareness of reading rate, and developing vocabulary. It is a good idea to help students practice these skills through class exercises and out of class assignments.

Depending on your students' needs, work with them to practice the strategies, identify their difficulties, and determine techniques that will help them improve their reading skills. Reading is critical to success in college. By helping your students develop these important reading strategies, they will begin to master textbook reading.

D. Suggested Outline for Addressing Topics in Chapter 7

STEP I: BEGIN WITH A LECTURE LAUNCHER OR ICEBREAKER ACTIVITY
STEP II: EMPLOY A VARIETY OF CLASSROOM ACTIVITIES
   a. Use the PowerPoint presentation from *Multimedia Manager 2007* resource
   b. Expand on key lesson themes
   c. Involve peer leaders
   d. Use chapter exercises
   e. Engage students in learning through case studies
STEP III: REVIEW & PREVIEW
   a. Address common questions and concerns about the topic
   b. Writing reflection
   c. Prepare for next class

Expanded Lesson Plan

STEP I: Lecture Launchers and Icebreakers

- Demonstrating the practice of previewing is a good way to begin a discussion about the material in this chapter. Ask students to take out this textbook and look at the first page of a chapter they haven't been assigned to read as yet (perhaps the next chapter you plan to teach). Have one student read the title of the chapter. Ask your students what they already know about this subject. Next, ask them to read through the introductory paragraphs as well as the chapter headings and subheadings. Remind them to note any study exercises at the end of the chapter. Now ask your students why taking these steps and the subsequent recommended previewing activities are important to their reading comprehension. Have students discuss how they normally read a chapter, and if they can see any differences between their usual method and the previewing one.

STEP II: Classroom Activities

a. Use the PowerPoint presentations in *Manager 2007* resource to complement your mini lecture.

b. Key Lesson Themes

- **Comparing Reading Strategies**
  This activity is designed to facilitate learning across the curriculum and to encourage students to apply reading strategies in all their courses:

  1. Ask students to make copies of one chapter of their text from each of three other courses they are currently taking.
  2. Have them highlight one chapter, annotate one, and take notes on the third.
  3. Ask students to do a writing assignment in which they evaluate which method assisted them most in retaining the chapter information and preparing for exams. Have them write about the pros and cons of each method.
  4. This approach should be meaningful to students because they are in essence studying for their other courses while completing your assignment.

- **Vocabulary Building**
  The following exercise is designed to illustrate that increasing one's vocabulary is an important part of the college reading process:

  1. Place students into groups of four. Tell them they are going to create a new vocabulary list of 10 words and definitions.
  2. Have each group member use this and other textbooks to create the list. It may be mostly subject-specific vocabulary they come up with, but that is okay.
  3. If you can provide them with a flip chart paper and markers, have them write out their lists. Members of each group can then present their list to the class.

c. Group Activities

- ### Exercise 7.3: Preparing to Read, Think, and Mark
  This exercise provides good practice for students. If time permits in class, give students a brief reading assignment from this text. Then ask them to process this exercise in pairs or small groups. Have them compare how they did, as well as whether or not their notes contain the same main ideas. Processing this exercise with the class and pointing out the main ideas will be useful for many students.

d. Peer Leader Assistance

- In American culture we often talk about whether or not someone likes to read. A good way to start this chapter might be to have a brief discussion with your students about their reading interests. Ask them to share if they like to read, what they like to read (novels, magazines, newspapers, etc.), and when they read. This will give you some insight into their thoughts about reading. You should also let the students know your reading material style and preferences.

e. Case Studies

Shondra
Shondra tells you that whenever she sits down to read her biology text she loses concentration or falls asleep. To her, it is *so boring*. Even when she does get through an entire chapter, she has no idea what she read. There is a lot of material included in each chapter. There are 25 chapters in this textbook that will be covered during the semester. The professor expects the class to read the textbook as well as take lecture notes. Both sets of information will be included on five tests they will have to take during the semester. Shondra has no idea how she will read all of the chapters, let alone how she will learn all the material. This class is a degree requirement for Shondra and one of four classes she is taking.

Discussion Questions:
1. What are Shondra's major issues concerning this class and her reading?
2. What are Shondra's options?
3. What suggestions would you make to assist Shondra?
4. What kind of strategies could help Shondra?
5. What other factors need to be considered besides how Shondra approaches her reading?

Barry
Barry is taking a philosophy course. The instructor has asked the class to do some research on the Internet to find three websites that give information about any of the philosophers they have discussed so far. Each student will bring up one website on the classroom computer and tell the class some new information they have learned. His

instructor instructs students that the websites must be credible and have accurate information. Barry has never done any research on the Internet. He doesn't know how to begin. This assignment is due in the next class.

Discussion Questions:
1. How would you suggest Barry get started?
2. What criteria could Barry use to evaluate the information on the websites he identifies?
3. How can Barry get more practice in doing research on the Internet?
4. What would alert Barry to the fact that a website may not be credible?
5. How would Barry cite these websites in a paper?

f. Chapter Exercises

- **Exercise 7.1: Previewing and Creating a Visual Map**
  Some students may consider this exercise "busy work," and for some this may be an accurate perception. However, the only way students can assess whether a strategy will work for them is by testing it out. This is a good homework assignment that they can bring to class and review in pairs or small groups.

- **Exercise 7.2: Doing What It Takes to Understand**
  Assign this exercise for homework, and as an additional assignment, ask them to evaluate the success of their exercise in their journals. You may also consider allotting class time for this exercise, and asking students to work in pairs.

STEP III: Review and Preview

REVIEW

a. Address Common Questions and Concerns of First-Year Students:

- *Why is there so much reading in college?*
  Answer: College takes a different approach to learning than many high school classes. As discussed in Chapter 4, students will need to be actively involved in their learning. This often means a lot of self-directed learning. Some instructors expect students to read a large amount of textbook material or even a wide range of articles and other materials outside of class. Help students grasp that they do not need to be frightened of these expectations and to understand that they can meet the challenge.

- *How can this reading method save me time? It looks like it takes more time.*
  Answer: Many students read their textbooks only to realize they have forgotten what they have read. Then they are still left to gather important textbook information to prepare for an exam. This method does take time and effort on the student's part; however, its benefits outweigh the time factor. Tell students this reading method will

give them a greater understanding of the material, increase their ability to focus and concentrate, and produce materials that will help them study for tests and quizzes.

- *Wouldn't it be easier just to take a speed-reading course?*
  Answer: While speed-reading can be helpful to increase reading rate and comprehension, there are many other considerations for reading a textbook. Tell your students that someone who speed-reads still needs to organize the material for later review and exams.

- *Why should I read the text if the instructor is going to lecture on it?*
  Answer: Students need to evaluate how closely the lecture and textbook materials coincide. Warn students not to skip classes even if the lecture seems to follow the text exactly. Explain to them they will miss other learning opportunities that take place in the classroom and may become disconnected from their instructor or classmates.

- *Why should I bother to take notes on my reading? I can always read the chapters again before the test.*
  Answer: Many students think they can read the chapters again before a test. In reality, the time constraints of college and the large amount of material to study for a test often prohibit this practice. Remind students that they must balance the work in one class with the work in their other classes, as well as outside commitments and responsibilities.

b. Writing Reflection

- Leave a few minutes at the end of class for students to complete the personal journal section on page 144.

PREVIEW FOR NEXT CLASS

Ask students to bring to the next class a copy of the exam where they received their lowest score.

E. Test Questions

Multiple Choice - choose ONE answer per question.

1. The first step in "attacking" a chapter in a text is
   a. previewing.
   b. outlining.
   c. reading.
   d. reviewing.

2. The first thing you should read when previewing a reading assignment is
   a. the chapter title.

b. the chapter outline.

c. the chapter summary.

d. the chapter assignments.

3. Developing a visual guide to a chapter is known as
   a. illustrating.
   b. chunking.
   c. mapping.
   d. outlining.

4. Dividing terms on a list into groups of five, seven, or nine is known as
   a. illustrating.
   b. chunking.
   c. mapping.
   d. outlining.

5. Flash cards are a great alternative to mapping for what kind of learners?
   a. Visual
   b. Aural
   c. Kinesthetic
   d. Interactive

6. In most sciences, it is best to
   a. outline chapters.
   b. memorize lectures.
   c. tape record lectures.
   d. highlight the textbook as you read through it.

7. _____ is an example of a social science course.
   a. Biology
   b. Public Speaking
   c. History
   d. Calculus

8. _____ is an example of a humanities course.
   a. Biology
   b. Astronomy
   c. Literature
   d. Calculus

9. What is an abstract?
   a. A paragraph-length summary of a longer piece
   b. An idea that is hard to conceptualize
   c. A listing of references used to write a book
   d. A listing of definitions

10. The final step in effective textbook reading is
    a. highlighting.
    b. reviewing.
    c. book marking.
    d. to copy it in your own handwriting.

True/False

11. It is best to highlight sentences as you read them for the first time.

12. A helpful strategy is to read the summary at the end of the textbook chapter before reading the chapter itself.

13. If you do not know a word in your reading, it's better to pass over it rather than interrupt your concentration.

14. Sometimes highlighting a text can provide you with a false sense of security.

15. You should never jot notes or comments in the margin of your books. It can later confuse and disorient you when you return to re-read and review.

Short Answer

16. Two common problems students have with textbooks are _____ and _____.

17. The final step in effective textbook reading is _____.

18. Name three basic vocabulary strategies mentioned in the chapter.

Essay

19. Do you think you will benefit most from highlighting, annotating, or outlining your text(s)? Why? Does it depend on the style of textbook or the subject matter? What other strategies do you intend to use to enhance comprehension and retention?

20. Describe some effective strategies for previewing chapters. Have you tried any of the methods presented in your text? If so, have they helped you read more efficiently? If not, which strategies do work for you?

CHAPTER 7 ANSWER KEY
1. a, p. 102
2. a, p. 102

3. c, p. 103
4. b, p. 103
5. d, p. 103
6. a, p. 133
7. c, p. 134
8. c, p. 134
9. a, p. 136
10. b, p.137
11. false, p. 104
12. true, p. 102
13. false, p. 110
14. true, p. 105
15. false, p. 105
16. trouble concentrating and not understanding the content, pp. 77-78
17. reviewing, p. 109
18. Answers will vary, pp.110-111

F. Web Resources

How to Read – http://www.ocean.edu/ReadColText/HowToReadCollegeTextDrJohnWeber.htm
Prepared by English professor Dr. John Webber, this site goes through the steps of proper college textbook reading, starting with previewing and finishing with a reminder that reading is an active process.

Concept Maps – http://www.psywww.com/mtsite/mindmaps.html
Mind Tools offers this feature, which explains how concept mapping improves note taking and reading comprehension. It includes sample maps, tips for improving mapping skills, and a link to concept mapping software, which can be downloaded for a free, 21-day trial.

Annotating Text – http://www.bucks.edu/~specpop/Access/annotating.htm
Most students don't know how to highlight effectively. This site suggests annotating texts, instead of simply highlighting them. It not only explains the best way to annotate information, but also offers a link to an example of a well-annotated passage.

A Word A Day – http://www.wordsmith.org/awad/
To encourage students to work on their vocabulary building skills, think about requiring them to register for the free version of this site. Each day they'll be e-mailed a new vocabulary word and its definition. You can monitor their comprehension of these words by giving weekly quizzes.

Reading Strategies -
http://www.mindtools.com/rdstratg.html
http://www.greece.k12.ny.us/instruction/ela/6-
12/Reading/Reading%20Strategies/reading%20strategies%20index.htm
http://www.mcps.k12.md.us/departments/isa/staff/abita/english/reading_strategies.htm

Inventory – http://www.dvc.edu/english/Learning_Resources/TextbookReadingInventory.htm
Print out this textbook reading inventory and give it to your students. Ask them to fill it out for one (or several) reading assignments to demonstrate how the reading methods proposed in this chapter really do increase comprehension.

G. For More Information

Elder, Janet. (2003). *Exercise your college reading skills: Developing more powerful comprehension.* New York: McGraw-Hill Humanities.

Langan, John. (1998). *Ten steps to advancing college reading skills (3rd ed).* West Berlin, NJ: Townsend Press.

Nist, Sherrie L. and Carole Mohr. (2002). *Advancing vocabulary skills (3rd ed).* West Berlin, NJ: Townsend Press.

Silvey, Deborah. (2002). *Reading from the inside out: Increasing your comprehension and enjoyment of college reading.* New York: Longman.

Wintner, Gene. (1995). *Practical college reading: Strategies for comprehension and vocabulary.* Burr Ridge, IL: Irwin Professional Publishing.

Chapter 8: Improving Your Memory

Ideas for Instruction and Instructor Training	Videos and CD-ROMs	Media Resources for Instructors	MEDIA RESOURCES FOR STUDENTS
Instructor's Manual (IM) Includes a brief lesson plan for Chapter 8, chapter objectives, lecture launchers, commentary on exercises in the book, and case studies. **Test Bank (in IM)** Multiple Choice, True/False, Short Answer and Essay Questions. Also available in ExamView® electronic format, which can be customized to fit your needs.	***10 Things Every Student Needs to Succeed in College* Video** 6-minute segment entitled "Enhancing Your Memory." **ExamView® CD-ROM** Computerized version of the Test Bank items for Chapter 8.	**JOININ™** Hand-held audience response device allows students immediate response to multiple-choice questions, polls, and interactive exercises. **Multimedia Manager 2007 CD-ROM** PowerPoint presentations, video clips, images, and web links help with assembly, editing, and presentation of multimedia lectures.	**iLrn® Pin-Coded Website** Contains self-assessments, electronic journals that encourage students to reflect on their progress, essay questions and exercises, and Test Your Knowledge interactive quizzes for Chapter 8. **InfoTrac® College Edition** May be bundled with text. *Keywords:* college success, liberal arts, goal setting, values, colleges, universities. **WebTutor™ Toolbox** Online course management tool for WebCT™ or Blackboard preloaded with text-specific content and media resources for Chapter 8.

A. Chapter Objectives

1. To learn how experts describe memory and its functions
2. To recognize myths about memory
3. To establish common-sense study methods that can produce greater learning and memory
4. To recognize the importance of having a good memory
5. To strengthen your ability to memorize

B. Timing of Chapter Coverage

In most university settings, the first round of exams typically occurs around the third week of the semester. At this point, students often recognize the need for improving their memory. This would be a good time to discuss some of the ideas in this chapter. Refer students to the appropriate campus resources and encourage them to use the strategies and aids outlined in the middle section of this chapter.

C. About This Chapter

This chapter offers solid strategies for improving your memory. Encourage students to understand memory and its functions. It is a good idea to help students practice these skills through class exercises and out of class assignments. Depending on your students' needs, work with them to practice the strategies, identify their difficulties, and to determine techniques that will help them improve their ability to memorize. The emphasis you give to the topics will depend on the make-up of the class. In addition, the chapter presents an opportunity to give the students a cooperative learning experience that is quite different from the discussions and exercises that flow from the other chapters.

D. Suggested Outline for Addressing Topics in Chapter 8

> **STEP I:**   BEGIN WITH A LECTURE LAUNCHER OR ICEBREAKER ACTIVITY
> **STEP II:** EMPLOY A VARIETY OF CLASSROOM ACTIVITIES
> > a.   Use the PowerPoint presentation from *Multimedia Manager 2007* resource
> > b.   Expand on key lesson themes
> > c.   Involve peer leaders
> > d.   Use chapter exercises
> > e.   Engage students in learning through case studies
>
> **STEP III**: REVIEW & PREVIEW
> > a.   Address common questions and concerns about the topic
> > b.   Writing reflection
> > c.   Prepare for next class

Expanded Lesson Plan

STEP I: Lecture Launchers and Icebreakers

- Before the class discusses the chapter, you might reflect on the significance of improving your own ability to improve your memorization as a professional, a consumer, a student, parent, and an informed citizen. Include your challenges and frustrations as well as your success stories.

- Starting the class with the exercise on page 157, Working Together, might work as a good icebreaker.

STEP II: Classroom Activities

a. Use the PowerPoint presentations in *Multimedia Manager 2007* resource to complement your mini lecture.

b. Key lesson themes

- **How memory works**
  http://www.thebrain.mcgill.ca/flash/d/d_07/d_07_cr/d_07_cr_tra/d_07_cr_tra.html
  Though not the focus of the chapter, you might want to spend some time addressing the topic of how memory works or direct your students to this web site that offers different

levels of explanation on this topic.

- **Memory strategies**
  Ask students to discuss memory strategies they have been taught or currently use. For example, many students have used acronyms for learning the colors of the rainbow (ROY G BIV). Discuss when you would use (or not use) certain techniques. For example, acronyms are good for remembering lists, but not good for learning new terms.

c. Group Activities

- Ask students to complete Exercise 8.1 and share their work in small groups.

- During lecture, ask students to propose memory techniques for learning the information being taught. Following the lecture, poll students on what they proposed.

d. Peer Leader Assistance

- Lead the class in completing Exercises 8.3 and 8.4. Since students probably already know each other's names, substitute names (Exercise 8.4) for their favorite foods.

e. Case Studies

Chethen
Chethen is required to take chemistry for his major in food science. In high school, Chethen excelled in his science classes and did not expect to be struggling in his college-level chemistry course. On his first exam, however, Chethen received a 47. Even with the curve, he did not crack a "D." Chethen finds himself becoming paralyzed by each subsequent quiz and exam and his grades do not improve. He needs to earn at least a "C" in this course to fulfill the requirement for his major. His midterm is approaching quickly and Chethen is afraid he will not only fail the test, but also the course.

Discussion Questions:
1. Why do you think Chethen is struggling so hard in chemistry when he did so well in his high school class?
2. If you were Chethen, how would you prepare for the upcoming midterm?
3. What are some steps Chethen could take to improve his grade?
4. How can Chethen reduce his anxiety when it comes to his chemistry quizzes and exams?

Alexia
Alexia tells you that whenever she sits down to prepare for her test, she loses concentration and gets overwhelmed. There is a lot of material included in each chapter of the textbook. There are 25 chapters in this textbook that will be covered during the semester. The professor plans to give essay and multiple choice questions. Alexia has no idea how she will read all of the chapters, let alone how she will learn all the material.

Discussion Questions:
1. What suggestions would you make to assist Alexia?
2. What kind of strategies could help Alexia?
3. What other factors need to be considered besides how Alexia approaches her memorization?

f. Chapter Exercises

- These are already interwoven in the lesson plan above.

STEP III: Review and Preview

REVIEW

a. Address Common Questions and Concerns of First-Year Students:

- *I am having problems getting good grades in courses like calculus and chemistry. Why am I required to take these courses when my goal is to earn a degree in business administration?*
  Answer: In today's marketplace, very few jobs *don't* require math and science. Your job is to illustrate to your students the real-world applications of these skills.

- *What should I do if I am unable to understand my instructor because he or she has a heavy foreign accent?*
  Answer: This is an instance where a note-taking study group would be beneficial. Comparing lecture notes with other students will help you fill in any "holes" you may have in your own. If you're still feeling lost, take advantage of the instructor's office hours and ask him or her to speak more slowly when explaining concepts. If there is a teaching or lab assistant for your course, you may also be able to approach him or her for additional assistance.

- *I feel totally lost in physics, I don't know what to memorize. Should I drop the class, or maybe get a tutor?*
  Answer: Before paying for a tutor, your students should make sure they've exhausted all of the free resources at their disposal. Has the student gone to the instructor's office hours? Has the student discussed the problems he or she is having with the teacher's assistant or lab assistant? Did the student join or form a study group? Does the school have a math lab where the student can get help with homework? Has the student attended any review sessions offered by the instructor? Supplemental materials and online resources may also help your student get a better grasp on difficult concepts.

b. Writing Reflection

- Leave a few minutes at the end of class for students to complete the Personal Journal section on p. 158.

PREVIEW FOR NEXT CLASS

Remind students that the next lesson on Tests and Exams is a very important one. They should read the chapter carefully in preparation for the next class.

E. Test Questions

Multiple Choice - choose ONE answer per question.

1. College is about deep learning; understanding the _____ behind the details
   a. previewing
   b. outlining and reading
   c. why and how
   d. none of the above

2. Information that is stored in short term memory is forgotten in less than
   a. 3 seconds.
   b. 3 minutes.
   c. 30 seconds.
   d. 30 minutes.

3. Long term memory is NOT
   a. procedural.
   b. semantic.
   c. mapping.
   d. episodic.

4. Which one is NOT a myth about memory?
   a. Some people are stuck with bad memories.
   b. There is no such thing as a photographic memory.
   c. Memory benefits from exercise.
   d. None of the above

5. The storage capacity of your memory is
   a. unlimited.
   b. aural.
   c. interactive.
   d. tapped.

6. The more you review your material, the more likely the material will
   a. become cluttered in your mind.
   b. be imprinted on your brain.

c. make you a visual learner.

d. none of the above

7. The text suggests that you do the following first:
   a. Get the big picture
   b. Know the details
   c. Fill in the blanks
   d. none of the above

8. Which is not a mnemonic to aid memory?
   a. Visual
   b. Aural
   c. Kinesthetic
   d. Interactive

9. The text recommends that you use a PDA as
   a. your main memory aid.
   b. a handy backup.
   c. your memory bank.
   d. all of the above

10. Learning piano sharps with the phrase "Francis can go down and eat bread" is a mnemonic technique called a
    a. rhyme.
    b. acrostic.
    c. acronym.
    d. visual aid.

True/False

11. All memory involves real learning.

12. Your semantic memory is used to recall word meanings or important dates.

13. How you approach memorization may depend on your learning style.

14. Overlearning the material can work against you.

15. Stress is a distraction to learning.

Short Answer

16. List two ways that technology can be a hindrance to memory.

17. List two reasons why mnemonics work.

18. What are four specific aids to improving your memory?

19. List three myths about memory.

20. What are three uses of short-term memory?

Essay

21. Do you think you will benefit most from using acronyms, acrostics, rhymes, or visual methods to aid your memory? Why? Does it depend on the style of textbook or the subject matter? What other strategies do you intend to use to enhance your memory?

22. Describe some specific aids to remember information (other than mnemonics). Have you tried any of the methods presented in your text? If so, have they helped you to remember more ? If not, which strategies do work for you?

23. The chapter lists several myths about memory. Were there any that you thought were true? Which ones? Now that you know these are not true, what changes do you foresee in the way you memorize and study for your tests?

24. Think of a situation in your own everyday life when you have a problem remembering. Apply some of the techniques, strategies and aids that were presented in this chapter. Be specific with questions to ask yourself, and steps to take.

25. What was the major lesson you learned from reading this chapter and/or from class lecture and discussion?

CHAPTER 8 ANSWER KEY
1. c, p. 147
2. c, p. 148
3. c, p. 148
4. b, p. 149
5. a, p. 149
6. b, p. 150
7. a, p. 151
8. b, p. 152
9. b, p. 154
10. b, p. 153
11. false, p. 147
12. true, p. 148
13. true, p. 150
14. false, p. 151
15. true, p. 152

F. Web Resources

Study Skills for Science Students – http://dept.dawsoncollege.qc.ca/lc/study-skills.html#science. This site is offered by Dawson's College. It is a collection of handouts geared toward science students. The online articles range from "Learning from Science Textbooks" to "Learning from Lab Notes" and "Preparing for Science Exams." It is a wonderful resource for your students.

Math.com – http://www.math.com/index.aspx
This site, geared toward both students and educators, offers some basic tutorials, as well as helpful calculators and converters. While the information found here won't be of much help to a higher-level math students, those who are taking a basic statistics course will be able to take advantage of these resources.

Concept Maps – http://www.psywww.com/mtsite/mindmaps.html
Mind Tools offers this feature, which explains how concept mapping improves note taking and reading comprehension. It includes sample maps, tips for improving mapping skills, and a link to concept mapping software, which can be download for a free 21-day trial.

Memory and Related Learning Principles
http://brain.web-us.com/memory/memory_and_related_learning_prin.htm
A very useful site. Most students don't know how to learn effectively. This site looks at effective strategies for learning course material.

Reading Strategies
http://www.mindtools.com/rdstratg.html

http://www.greece.k12.ny.us/instruction/ela/6-12/Reading/Reading%20Strategies/reading%20strategies%20index.htm

http://www.mcps.k12.md.us/departments/isa/staff/abita/english/reading_strategies.htm

G. For More Information

Elder, Janet. (2003). *Exercise your college reading skills: Developing more powerful comprehension.* New York: McGraw-Hill Humanities.

Koomey, Jonathan G. and Chris Calwell. (2003). *Turning numbers into knowledge: Mastering the art of problem solving.* Oakland, CA: Analytics Press.

Learning for success. Toronto: Harcourt Brace Jovanovich, 1990.

MacFarlane, Polly, and Sandra Hodson. *Studying effectively and efficiently: An integrated system.* Toronto: University of Toronto, 1983.

Ornstein, Robert. (1997). *The right mind*, Orlando, FL: Harcourt Brace.

Post, Beverly and Sandra Eads. (1998). *Logic, anyone?* White Plains, NY: Dale Seymour Press.

Silvey, Deborah. (2002). *Reading from the inside out: Increasing your comprehension and enjoyment of college reading.* New York: Longman

Tallal, Paula. (2000). Experimental studies of language learning impairments: From research to remediation. In Bishop, D. V. M., & Leonard, L. B. (Eds.), *Speech and language impairments in children: Causes, characteristics, intervention, and outcome.* Hove, UK: Psychology Press.

Wintner, Gene. (1995). *Practical college reading: Strategies for comprehension and vocabulary.* Burr Ridge, IL: Irwin Professional Publishing.

Chapter 9: Taking Exams and Tests

By Jeanne L. Higbee, Professor and Faculty Chair, Center for Research on Developmental Education and Urban Literacy, General College, University of Minnesota

Ideas for Instruction and Instructor Training	Videos and CD-ROMs	Media Resources for Instructors	Media Resources for Students
Instructor's Manual (IM) Includes a brief lesson plan for Chapter 9, chapter objectives, lecture launchers, commentary on exercises in the book, and case studies. **Test Bank (in IM)** Multiple Choice, True/False, Short Answer and Essay Questions. Also available in ExamView® electronic format, which can be customized to fit your needs.	***10 Things Every Student Needs to Know to Study Video*** 6-minute segment entitled "Taking a Test." **ExamView® CD-ROM** Computerized version of the Test Bank items for Chapter 9.	JoinIn™ Hand-held audience response device allows students immediate response to multiple-choice questions, polls, and interactive exercises. **Multimedia Manager 2007 CD-ROM** PowerPoint presentations, video clips, images, and web links help with assembly, editing, and presentation of multimedia lectures.	**iLrn® Pin-Coded Website** Contains self-assessments, electronic journals that encourage students to reflect on their progress, essay questions and exercises, and Test Your Knowledge interactive quizzes for chapter 9. **InfoTrac® College Edition** May be bundled with text. *Keywords:* college success, liberal arts, goal setting, values, colleges, universities. **WebTutor™ Toolbox** Online course management tool for WebCT™ or Blackboard preloaded with text-specific content and media resources for Chapter 9.

A. Chapter Objectives

1. To demonstrate that all of the study skills taught in previous chapters facilitate preparation for tests
2. To teach strategies for preparing for and taking different types of exams
3. To illustrate how academic dishonesty hurts both the student and the academic community
4. To understand what behaviors constitute academic dishonesty
5. To explain ways to aid memory
6. To encourage the design of an exam study plan
7. To demonstrate different types of exam study tools

B. Timing of Chapter Coverage

Test taking is a critical skill that students will need to master. They may encounter differences in testing from what they were used to in high school. It is suggested that this chapter be taught as soon as possible after you've addressed study skills and definitely before the first round of major exams occur.

C. About This Chapter

First-year students often have unrealistic expectations. Each student is different. Some strategies are more effective for some students than for others. There will always be some students who will be successful with what appears to be relatively little effort in some subjects. Other students will follow all the suggestions in this book and still be disappointed with their grades. These students need to learn from their test experiences in order to be better prepared in the future.

Students who use the methods suggested in the previous chapters are likely to be successful on exams. It is imperative that students understand that studying for exams begins on the first day of class. Encouraging students to form study groups can add to their success. A well-chosen study group provides students with the opportunity to assess their understanding of the material. Group discussions confirm or deny understanding. The study group also provides an opportunity to fill in any blanks that may exist, through either misunderstanding, oversight, or absence. Also, different students will bring different approaches to studying, which can create a desirable richness to the group. Finally, the will of the group to study can overcome individual procrastination.

The key to effective study groups is their composition. Students should invite others based on their serious commitment to doing well. Every member of a study group should make a contribution and those who do not should be asked to leave.

If you time the coverage of this chapter carefully, you will be able to discuss test preparation at about the time your first-year students are preparing to take their first major exams. This is also a good time to talk about test anxiety; unfortunately some students are not able to demonstrate their knowledge on exams because they fall prey to their fears about testing. Encourage those students who struggle with test anxiety to seek help to change this. For some of them, improving their study tools and memory strategies will help with some of the anxiety. Talking with instructors, tutors, and classmates can also be helpful. In cases like this, developing a positive relationship with faculty can be so important to a student's success.

Today's students are fully aware that some students cheat. However, they may equate academic dishonesty with copying another student's test answers or having another student write their papers. They may not be aware of other behaviors that constitute cheating. Discussing real examples of unauthorized assistance and other situations that may be construed as academic dishonesty can aid students in avoiding potential difficulties. Students are often much more open to this type of discussion than a lecture on ethical issues.

It will be important that you help students to see that test preparation is a culmination of their ongoing study habits. Encourage them to develop a study system with both test taking and learning as the main objectives. Through the chapter information and exercises, have your students explore their past study strategies that lead up to exams and look for ways to make improvements on that.

D. Suggested Outline for Addressing Topics in Chapter 9

> **STEP I:** BEGIN WITH A LECTURE LAUNCHER OR ICEBREAKER ACTIVITY
> **STEP II:** EMPLOY A VARIETY OF CLASSROOM ACTIVITIES
>   a. Use the PowerPoint presentation from *Multimedia Manager 2007* resource
>   b. Expand on key lesson themes
>   c. Involve peer leaders
>   d. Use chapter exercises
>   e. Engage students in learning through case studies
> **STEP III:** REVIEW & PREVIEW
>   a. Address common questions and concerns about the topic
>   b. Writing reflection
>   c. Prepare for next class

Expanded Lesson Plan

STEP I: *Lecture Launchers and Icebreakers*

- You may find that your students' expectations of college tests and exams are somewhat different than those in high school. Begin by asking students to discuss the differences they are encountering in college tests. They may note such things as types of exams, amount of material on each exam, and deciding on what to study for an exam. Having this discussion with students will help them to identify these differences and allow them to determine how they will make adjustments in exam preparation.

- Lead an in-class discussion on cheating. Ask your students to brainstorm, either as a group or individually, about how they would define cheating in an academic setting. Ask the students to consider different scenarios, including topics like plagiarism from books and the web, using papers or homework turned in previously by other students and cheating during exams. Try to encourage the students to think about situations in which they were unsure about the difference between cheating and "borrowing" ideas from books or other sources.

STEP II: *Classroom Activities*

a. Use the PowerPoint presentations in *Multimedia Manager 2007* resource to complement your mini lecture.

b. Key Lesson Themes

- **Essay Exams**
  Use this activity to show students a method of planning for essay-based exams and to

give students practice on how to prepare for essay test questions:

1. Using the list of key task words in the chapter, ask groups to prepare six or seven potential essay questions from their notes.
2. Have each student choose one of the questions and prepare a brief outline to share with the other students.
3. Next, ask students to critique each other's outlines.
4. Bring in concrete essay questions illustrating the different key task words. Do not assume that students will understand them without examples.

- **Exam Questions**
  Use this activity to give students practice preparing for other common types of exam questions:

  1. Use the test construction strategy similar to the one suggested for essay (above).
  2. Ask each student to construct ten objective questions for one of the chapters of this text.
  3. Then, test the students using the questions they have constructed.

- **Test Anxiety**
  Invite a counselor or student affairs professional to share their expertise and provide practical ways to control or overcome test anxiety.

c. Group Activities

- Use the activities in the margins of page 162 to generate discussion about the importance of one being physically and emotionally prepared for an exam.

- Ask students to brainstorm pros and cons about study groups. Have the groups report back to the class. Ask the class to offer suggestions on how to change the cons into pros.

- Ask students to work with a partner to review the mind map in figure 9.1. Ask each to select a chapter from a textbook they are currently reading in a course. Students can use transparencies to showcase their mind maps in class.

d. Peer Leader Assistance

- You can share your personal experiences with test anxieties. What memories do you have with high stake tests: ACT, SAT,GRE etc.?

- Spend sometime addressing the key points that are raised in the margins of your text on pages 171-174. This might be more meaningful to freshmen if they hear these pointers from another student.

e. Case Studies

Christopher

Christopher asks to talk to his professor about the results of his first exam in his American History class. Christopher is a pre-law major, and his success in this course is very important to him. He tells the professor that he loves history and always earned the highest grades in his history classes in high school. Christopher has always used the reading, note taking, and test-preparation strategies he learned in class, and had thought he was well prepared for the history exam. However, he acknowledges that he guessed at many of the items on the multiple-choice part of the exam. He thought he had done well on the essay, but he scored only 30 out of the 50 possible points. Overall, Christopher received a grade of 63 out of 100 points.

Discussion Questions:
1. How would you respond to Christopher?
2. What could have gone wrong with Christopher's test preparation?
3. What could have gone wrong during the exam?
4. What suggestions do you have for Christopher?
5. What exam preparation system would you suggest that Christopher utilize for his next exam?

An-Yi

An-Yi is getting close to the deadline for her 10-page term paper in her environmental studies class. She has had eight weeks to research and write the paper and now she finds herself with another three days left before it is due. She finds the class boring and doesn't see how it relates to her major, business. An-Yi got her topic approved by her instructor during the first week as required, but she hasn't done a thing since then. She is panicking, but still doesn't have the motivation to write the paper. One of An-Yi's close friends suggests a website where you can purchase research papers on any topic. She tells An-Yi to buy one and modify it a little to make it her own work. An-Yi is seriously considering doing this.

Discussion Questions:
1. What are An-Yi's important issues here?
2. What suggestions do you have for An-Yi?
3. What alternatives does An-Yi have?
4. If An-Yi purchases and modifies a paper, would this be considered cheating?
5. What consequences would An-Yi face if this is considered cheating?

f. Chapter Exercises

- #### Exercise 9.1: Designing an Exam Plan
  Designing an exam plan is an extremely useful exercise for many students, especially if they have not had much structure around preparing for and taking exams. This makes a good individual project as well as group assignment. In small groups, have students

design a plan for the next exam in your class. The group members can present their plan to the class, sharing their strategies and why they designed that particular plan.

- **Exercise 9.2: Forming a Study Group**
  Assign this exercise as homework, perhaps as an additional journal entry. You can also have students bring their written answers to class and share their responses in small groups.

- **Exercise 9.3: Sharpening Your Memory**
  Memory exercises can be extremely helpful to some students. Consider demonstrating the techniques in class, assigning practice of them out of class, and asking students to turn in a written assessment of how helpful each technique was. You can also tie in further discussion about different learning preferences (i.e., interactive learners might benefit most from flashcard exercises).

STEP III: Review and Preview

REVIEW

a. Address Common Questions and Concerns of First-Year Students:

- *How do I know what kind of questions the teacher will ask on the test?*
  Answer: Some instructors are very clear about the types of questions that will be on a test. Others are not. Students will have to listen carefully in the classroom for this information. If the instructor is not specific, they can talk with the instructor after class or during office hours, as well as consult their classmates for additional insight.

- *How can I be sure I am studying the right things?*
  Answer: Again, some instructors will be very clear about the material a particular test will cover, while others may not. Students may find that some instructors give a review before a test and may even hand out a study outline. Checking with reliable classmates may often help students if they are unsure. Emphasize to students that being actively involved in their own learning will help with knowing what to study for a test.

- *Why not pull an all-nighter? I always do better under pressure.*
  Answer: Cutting back on sleep is not a good idea because it deprives the brain of the rest it needs to work at full power. Students need sleep to do their best critical thinking and remain alert during exams. Encourage them to maintain their regular sleep routines before exams.

- *How will I ever learn six weeks' worth of information in time to pass this test?*
  Answer: Preparing for exams should actually start on the first day of the term. Lecture notes, reading information, and doing homework are all part of the preparation. Explain to students that organizing course materials and good time management will aid their learning and are best if done right from the start of class, not one week or a few days

before a test. Studying and organizing material right before a test may be too late to learn all the material and perform well on the test.

- ***Is it cheating if I didn't intend to cheat?***
  Answer: Cheating is usually cheating even if you didn't mean to. Students must be aware of both institutional policies and their instructors' rules on academic conduct. Ignorance of the rules is not acceptable. Students may be risking not only an "F" on a test or in a course, but other consequences as well, such as expulsion. Talking about academic integrity is important here.

- ***Is it okay to work together on a take-home math exam? In class the teacher always has us solve problems in small groups.***
  Answer: Unless specifically told that it is okay to collaborate, this is usually not acceptable. Even with take-home exams, instructors still expect that students will do their own work and are looking to evaluate them on just that. When in doubt, tell students to check with the instructor.

- ***If there are different opinions on what cheating is, how can I be held responsible?***
  Answer: Different institutions do have different policies about the types of academic misconduct. However, students must realize that they are responsible for knowing exactly what the institutional policies are and the corresponding consequences. Encourage students to be proactive in reducing any problems that may arise by knowing the rules and setting clear boundaries for themselves.

b. Writing Reflection

- Use the questions on page 182 to allow students to express their reactions regarding the material that was covered in this chapter.

PREVIEW FOR NEXT CLASS
Ask students to complete Exercise 10.4 and be prepared to have their classmates critique their presentation. Or, have each student choose a topic on which to give a short speech. In the next class when they deliver their speeches, record them using a camcorder or other such device.

E. Test Questions

Multiple Choice - choose ONE answer per question.

1. Someone who takes another person's ideas or work and passes it off as their own has
   a. cheated.
   b. plagiarized.
   c. committed fraud.
   d. exhibited ignorance.

2. When studying for an exam, what's the maximum number of caffeinated drinks recommended?
   a. 0
   b. 2
   c. 4
   d. There is no recommended limit.

3. When it comes to studying, exercise does all of the following EXCEPT
   a. reduces stress.
   b. improves clarity.
   c. limits need for sleep.
   d. provides positive study breaks.

4. A design for test preparation is commonly referred to as a(n)
   a. mind map.
   b. review sheet.
   c. flashcard.
   d. exam plan.

5. Questions containing words like often and frequently suggest what?
   a. The statement may be true.
   b. The statement is always true.
   c. The statement may be false.
   d. The statement is always false.

6. Questions containing words like always, never, and only suggest what?
   a. The statement may be true.
   b. The statement is always true.
   c. The statement may be false.
   d. The statement is always false.

7. Open-book and open-notes test are usually _____ other exams.
   a. more difficult than
   b. easier than
   c. the same as
   d. none of the above

8. Take-home tests are usually_____ in-class tests.
   a. more difficult than
   b. easier than
   c. the same as
   d. none of the above

9. The technique of using self-messages that are encouraging rather than stress-provoking is called
   a. review sheet.
   b. acing a test.
   c. cognitive restructuring.
   d. none of the above

10. Instructors tend to prefer essay exams because they promote
    a. mind maps.
    b. memorization.
    c. higher-order critical thinking.
    d. none of the above

True/False:

11. Purchasing a term paper on the Web is cheating, but asking your roommate to rewrite your awkward sentences is not.

12. As long as you're not using a direct quote, you do not need to cite the source of the material.

13. Tutoring is only for students who are failing or in danger of failing a class.

14. Always respond T to a true/false question that contains the word "always."

15. On an essay exam, it's easy to misread the questions.

Short Answer

16. List five of the key task words discussed in your text.

17. Define the five terms you listed in question 11.

18. Give two tips for successful test taking.

19. Give three tips for answering essay questions.

20. What are some of the consequences of cheating in an academic setting?

Essay Questions

21. In your opinion, why do colleges and universities have such strict policies regarding academic honesty? What do you think of your school's policy? How would you revise/improve it?

22. Your final exam in sociology will be all essay questions. You will have three hours to respond to your choice of six essays out of ten options provided. List and describe the steps for your strategy for completing this exam.

23. Describe how and why doing well on exams can depend on physical and emotional preparation.

24. Give advice to a student who is flunking on her exams because of test anxieties. Help this student understand the sources, identify the symptoms, and offer strategies for combating test anxieties.

25. Now that you have studied this chapter on test-taking, what have you identified that is keeping you from performing at your peak level academically? What changes do you propose to make? What are some of the outcomes you envision you'll receive from making these changes?

CHAPTER 9 ANSWER KEY

1. b, p. 162
2. c, p. 162
3. d, p. 165
4. a, p. 173
5. c, p. 173
6. a, p. 175
7. a, p. 176
8. c, p. 169
9. c, p. 170
10. false, p. 176
11. false, p. 176
12. false, p. 163
13. false, p. 173
14. true, p. 172
15. Answers will vary, pp. 173-174
16. Answers will vary, pp. 173-174
17. Answers will vary, p. 170

F. Web Resources

Plagiarism – http://www.indiana.edu/~wts/pamphlets.shtml
From Indiana University comes this page, which explains what exactly constitutes plagiarism, as well as how to recognize and avoid it.

Preparing for Tests – http://www.ucs.umn.edu/lasc/handouts/preptests.html
The University of Minnesota's Counseling and Consulting Services center offers a very thorough take on how to best prepare for an exam. It includes a blank "inventory" students can fill out to ascertain "where they are" in terms of prepping for a specific test.

Test-Taking Strategies -
http://www.d.umn.edu/student/loon/acad/strat/test_take.html
http://www.mtsu.edu/~studskl/teststrat.html
http://www.eop.mu.edu/study/

Analyzing T & F Questions – http://www.ucs.umn.edu/lasc/handouts/analizingtf.html
This great list of tips for answering true/false exam questions is delivered as (what else?) a true/false exam.

Taking Multiple-Choice Tests – http://core.ecu.edu/psyc/wuenschk/TestTips.htm
More test-taking tips can be found on this page, which focuses on how to improve success when facing multiple-choice questions.

Test Anxiety – http://www.counsel.ufl.edu/selfHelp/testAnxiety.asp
Test anxiety can be crippling to students. To help them overcome their test-taking fears, direct them to this site and discuss how things like improving self-esteem, which seem totally unrelated to exams, will help improve their performance.

G. For More Information

Buzan, Tony. (2003). *How to mind map: Make the most of your mind and learn to create, organize, and plan.* New York: Thorsons Pub.

Educational Testing Service. (2004). *Reducing test anxiety (Praxis study guides).* Princeton, NJ: Author.

Myers, Judith N. (2000). *The secrets of taking any test (2ⁿᵈ ed).* San Diego, CA: Learning Express, Inc.

Robinson, Adam. (1993). *What smart students know: Maximum grades, optimum learning, minimum time.* New York: Three Rivers Press.

Rozakis, Laurie. (2002). *Test taking strategies & study skills for the utterly confused.* New York: McGraw-Hill Trade.

Chapter 10: Effective Writing and Speaking

Ideas for Instruction and Instructor Training	Videos and CD-ROMs	Media Resources for Instructors	MEDIA RESOURCES FOR STUDENTS
Instructor's Manual (IM) Includes a brief lesson plan for Chapter 10, chapter objectives, lecture launchers, commentary on exercises in the book, and case studies. **Test Bank (in IM)** Multiple Choice, True/False, Short Answer and Essay Questions. Also available in ExamView® electronic format, which can be customized to fit your needs.	***10 Things Every Student Needs to Succeed in College* Video** 6-minute segment entitled "Communicate Well: Public Speaking/Written Expression." **ExamView® CD-ROM** Computerized version of the Test Bank items for Chapter 10.	**JOININ™** Hand-held audience response device allows students immediate response to multiple-choice questions, polls, and interactive exercises. **Multimedia Manager 2007 CD-ROM** PowerPoint presentations, video clips, images, and web links help with assembly, editing, and presentation of multimedia lectures.	**iLrn® Pin-Coded Website** Contains self-assessments, electronic journals that encourage students to reflect on their progress, essay questions and exercises, and Test Your Knowledge interactive quizzes for Chapter 10. **InfoTrac® College Edition** May be bundled with text. *Keywords:* college success, liberal arts, goal setting, values, colleges, universities. **WebTutor™ Toolbox** Online course management tool for WebCT™ or Blackboard preloaded with text-specific content and media resources for Chapter 10.

A. Chapter Objectives

1. To demonstrate the importance of writing to communicate
2. To delineate three key sequential steps in the writing process
3. To demystify the writing process
4. To make students aware of the importance of speaking in college and life success
5. To lower students' anxiety about public speaking
6. To acquaint students with six important steps in preparing a successful speech
7. To help students gain impromptu speaking skills – the ability to think on their feet
8. To make speaking fun and challenging through the use of lively in-class exercises

B. Timing of Chapter Coverage

The writing portion of this chapter warrants attention early in the term. In fact, you might integrate the writing concepts in this chapter with the earlier chapters on study skills, for the obvious reason that students who learn to put thoughts on paper clearly tend to be better at absorbing material and explaining material on tests.

The chapter also focuses on two aspects of speaking: prepared speeches and impromptu speaking. You may want to break the speaking portion into these two components and use them at separate times during the term. While it is important to get students comfortable with "informal" speaking in class immediately, this part of the chapter is probably best used around the middle of the term. First-year students often have high anxiety about formal speaking assignments, particularly at the start of the course when they do not know their classmates. The purpose of this section of the chapter is not to teach students everything they need to know about public speaking. However, if a speaking component is to be included in the course (which we highly recommend), students must be provided with strategies to help them complete the assignment successfully.

C. About This Chapter

Writing

You will find that first-year students tend to fall into one of three categories when it comes to writing: the deluded, the helpless, and the true writers. The deluded have received high marks on papers in high school and are convinced that there is nothing more to learn about writing. Sadly, this is often far from the case. Many students will claim that they learned some unbreakable rules about writing that you seem to be breaking. For example: "An essay should contain only five paragraphs: a thesis statement, four points, and a conclusion." Or, "Never use the first or second person in writing." What they have missed, perhaps, is that writing style depends to a large extent on the audience one is writing for. This group will find their mediocre grades shocking and may go so far as to let you know how well they did in high school. The helpless haven't received those high grades, and perhaps that's a blessing. While they are probably convinced that they will never be good writers, these students represent fertile territory for writing instruction. Coach them gently; along with your criticisms, find something positive to write on every paper. Be encouraging. This, of course, applies to the first group as well. Finally, we come to the true writers. You can expect to get wonderful work from these folks who, seemingly, have overcome what may have been inadequate writing instruction and developed a style of their own. Although you will still find things to critique, face it, anyone's writing can always be improved, you will love reading their papers.

Be certain to introduce writing as a means of motivating thinking. Use the suggestions in the chapter to get them started. Above all, try to convince them that good writing can open doors for them throughout their lives. For example, have you ever tried to read a poorly written resume?

Speaking

Typically, first-year students have considerable anxiety about speaking in front of others. They see public speaking as cause for extreme self-consciousness, rather than as an opportunity to command the attention of others and communicate the totality of their thoughts. Normal dialog denies speakers the full extent of these opportunities, because give and take is required. Conversational speakers who command attention and monopolize the interaction are considered to be lacking in social skills. Public speakers, on the other hand, are expected to command and control. You can present these ideas as advantages of public speaking. Keep the following goals in mind in helping students manage their anxiety:

- Recast public speaking as "multiple conversations."
- Redefine public speaking as a natural part of life.

- Redirect students' anxieties for use as productive energy.

Recasting Public Speaking

Help students rethink public speaking as multiple "conversations" occurring simultaneously. Encourage students to think of themselves speaking to each individual in the class as they would during normal conversation, rather than speaking to a group of people. Students often think they must play a role while speaking in front of others—a role with which they are not comfortable. Remind them that speakers should be themselves, rather than playing the role of orator. It's important to let their personalities shine through while speaking publicly. Simply reporting information isn't enough; audiences are interested in speakers as people.

Redefining Public Speaking

Help students understand that when we come right down to it, all speaking is public speaking. Whenever we speak, we do so in public. Few of us do much speaking in private. In other words, public speaking should be considered a continual way of life rather than a "one-shot" event.

Redirecting Anxiety

Remind students that experiencing anxiety while speaking in front of others is normal. Anxiety means that students care about what they're doing and want to do well. Anxiety can be harnessed as productive energy if they follow the advice on preparation and rehearsal presented in the chapter. Of course, students with excessive anxiety may require extra coaching from you or a referral to the communication department or speech lab on campus, if available. Like swimming, speaking is the kind of skill that can only be learned by doing. Reading about speaking and discussing how to give a speech must be combined with speaking opportunities. Keep in mind that evaluating public speaking is tricky. Speaking is an egocentric activity, and instructors must be careful to provide helpful feedback without bruising fragile egos. Producing a speech is comparable to creating a work of art; identifying areas for improvement must be done supportively, and students' self-esteem must be protected. If the entire class is to provide feedback following speeches, it's important to set guidelines and encourage constructive rather than destructive comments from the class. Some instructors elect to provide only positive feedback in public; they communicate negative comments supportively in one-on-one coaching sessions after class. However you choose to proceed, sensitivity is key.

The most effective way to improve speaking skills is to allow students to view themselves on videotape. If you have the opportunity to videotape students' speeches yourself or can have the media department or a student assistant do so, students can see and hear speaking errors themselves and self-improvement can be dramatic.

D. Suggested Outline for Addressing Topics in Chapter 10

STEP I: BEGIN WITH A LECTURE LAUNCHER OR ICEBREAKER ACTIVITY
STEP II: EMPLOY A VARIETY OF CLASSROOM ACTIVITIES
      a.   Use PowerPoint presentation from *Multimedia Manager 2007* resource
      b.   Expand on key lesson themes
      c.   Involve peer leaders
      d.   Use chapter exercises
      e.   Engage students in learning through case studies
STEP III: REVIEW & PREVIEW
      a.   Address common questions and concerns about the topic
      b.   Writing reflection
      c.   Prepare for next class

Expanded Lesson Plan

STEP I: Lecture Launchers and Icebreakers

- Have your students review some famous speeches, first in the written form and then in audio or video form. Have them compare both versions and analyze the strengths and possible weaknesses of each. This will not only introduce your students to the chapter material, it will provide them with a strong illustration of the importance of both the written and spoken word.

- Ask for half a dozen volunteers. Hand each one a folded slip of paper with a certain posture written on it (arms folded across chest, head tilted, etc.). Next, ask each student to repeat the same sentence (of your choosing) using the assigned posture. Have your class guess which attitude is implied by which posture. This will lead to a discussion on the importance of body language. You may also want to ask your students to decode the tone of voice used by your volunteers. For example, did they automatically adjust their normal tone to match their assigned posture?

STEP II: Classroom Activities

a. Use the PowerPoint presentations in *Multimedia Manager 2007* to complement your mini lecture.

b. Expand on key lesson themes

- **Freewriting**
  To get students into the habit of using freewriting, open the class meeting with a short

freewriting session (perhaps five minutes) on a topic related to the chapter. Continue to do this week after week to encourage students to regularly reflect on the reading, the course, and their own perspectives.

- **Using Video to Improve Student Speeches**
  In preparation for this chapter, have each student choose a topic on which to give a short speech. On the day that the students deliver the speeches, record them using a camcorder. The following session, ask your students what makes for a successful speech. Decide as a class which criteria are most important. Next, play the video for your class.

c. Group Activities

- Using tape recorded video, have the students critique each speech on the basis of the criteria they decided on. As a final step, you may ask each student to write a brief response to the entire process, from delivering the speech to having it critiqued by fellow classmates. Ask them to assess their strengths and weakness as a speechmaker. This can be an eye-opener for many students. If they are willing, have them turn their papers in or read them to the class. More importantly, collect the papers they wrote about the experience. Ask them to share them with the rest of the class and to come to some conclusion about the relative value of the exercise and how they might use it to improve their public speaking.

d. Peer Leader Assistance
- In addition to actively participating in the activities surrounding this topic, peer leaders should make sure that props and logical arrangements for these activities are scheduled ahead of time.

e. Case Studies

Daphne
In high school, Daphne excelled in English, earning mostly "A"s on her papers. She had a knack for figuring out what teachers wanted to read and knew how to deliver the material in a clean, articulate fashion. So Daphne wasn't all that concerned when she had her first big essay due in her freshman composition class. She started the paper three nights before it was due, finished it the following day, and turned the essay in early. She was confident that she would receive another "A."

When she got her essay back, however, Daphne was dismayed to see that she had only earned a "C." Her instructor's comments noted a lack of original thought, disorganized structure, and several typos as the reasons for the lower than expected grade. Daphne was crushed. Why were her usual writing methods failing her now? When the next essay came up, Daphne found herself paralyzed by fear. She didn't know what to write or how to write it. On top of that, she wasn't sure how she should structure the paper once she chose a topic. Eventually, she "borrowed" a topic from her roommate. After waiting until the night before the paper was due, Daphne repeated the process she used on the first paper, hoping this time her instructor would be more generous with the grades.

Discussion Questions:
1. What were some of the things Daphne did wrong in writing the first paper? The second?
2. What steps should Daphne take if she truly wants to write "A" papers?
3. How could Daphne have better prepared herself for that second paper? Have you ever had writer's block? What did you do to get over it?

Jake

For his college success course, Jake was assigned to do a 10-minute PowerPoint presentation on his research topic. He had three weeks to prepare—a good length of time. He projected his schedule for the next three weeks in his head. In addition to soccer finals, his parents were flying in for a visit, and the following week his high school girlfriend was driving up for a visit as well. Along with his other classes, these important events were likely to take up some time. But Jake wasn't concerned. He made a mental note to run some topic ideas by his father and to ask his girlfriend (who was a whiz at PowerPoint) for some help.

Despite Jake's "planning," the days clicked by, visits came and went, and the speech never seemed to get done. Jake had never considered himself to be very good at public speaking, and the thought of taking on such a big project was overwhelming. The night before, he went through a few last-minute motions doing Internet research and putting together a few slides. It wasn't a valiant attempt; in fact, Jake knew it was some of the worst work he'd ever done. But he was finished, and that was what mattered most in Jake's head.

Discussion Questions:
1. Have you ever felt as Jake did in this case study? What was worrying Jake? In your own experience, what worried you?
2. Why does procrastination sometimes appear to be such an attractive option? What kinds of things do we tell ourselves about doing the work later?
3. Was fear an issue in Jake's procrastination? Should Jake have gone to Professor Stanley and explained his fear of public speaking?
4. If you had been Jake, what would you have done to make the project less threatening and more manageable?

f. Chapter Exercises

Exercise 10.1: Engage by Writing
In class, have students write how the exercise helped them—or how it didn't.

Exercise 10.2: The Power of Focused Observation

This can be an eye-opener for many students. If they are willing, have them turn their papers in or read them to the class. More importantly, collect the papers they wrote *about* the experience. Ask them to also share them with the rest of the class and to come to some conclusion about the relative value of the exercise and how they might use it to improve their writing assignments in all classes.

Exercise 10.3: Parallels
This exercise is perhaps best used as a journal assignment.

Exercise 10.4: PowerPoint Presentation
As the graphics software industry standard in an estimated 95 percent of U.S. companies, PowerPoint is an effective tool that can be learned easily in the first-year seminar course. Begin with a low-threat assignment about a familiar subject, possibly the student him or herself, and watch them go! They become proficient quickly and enjoy using their technological skills. As a byproduct, the tool helps students understand the process of organizing presentations.

Exercise 10.5: Chiseled-in-Stone Speech
First-year students often respond favorably to visual demonstrations and to "extreme" examples used to make a point. By disallowing *any* movement whatsoever while delivering a speech, students begin to realize that physical animation while communicating is a natural predisposition, one that should be cultivated as an important component of dynamism in public speaking.

STEP III: Review and Preview

REVIEW

a. Address Common Questions and Concerns of First-Year Students:

- *I already know how to write. Why do I have to practice an approach that I don't like?*

  Answer: Writing is a powerful tool of communication. It's also a skill students will need for the rest of their lives. The approach taught in this chapter emphasizes organization and revision, two steps most first-year students think they can skip. Explain to them that even published authors use this process. You must also impress upon them that no matter how brilliant they are as students, if they do not know how to articulate their thoughts both in writing and verbally, know one will be able to measure just how brilliant they are.

- *I'll never be a good writer. My major is math (or science, or engineering, or…) and I won't need to write.*
  Answer: Again, writing is a basic life skill. Although students who are oriented toward math and sciences may never grow to love the writing process, they must learn to master it. To convert skeptical students, give them examples of how good writing

skills are an asset in math- and science-related careers. You may also try to relate the writing process to something they are more comfortable with, such as a formula. By doing this, you are demystifying the writing process, and making it more accessible to these students.

- *Why do I have to know how to give a speech? I'm not planning on being a politician.*
  Answer: Being able to articulate thoughts verbally is every bit as important as being able to do so in writing. Again, make sure your students are aware of how good speaking skills will aid them in practical ways, such as on job interviews.

- *When I give a speech, my heart pounds and my knees knock. How can I keep from being nervous?*
  Answer: Fear of public speaking is natural, especially among first-year students. In addition to reviewing the section "Speaking in Public Need Not Be Scary" (page 139), direct them to Chapter 17, "Stress Management." There they will find information on reducing anxiety.

- *Should I memorize my speech? What kind of notes do I need?*
  Answer: Memorizing a speech often leads to a flat delivery. It is better for students to create an outline of key points they want to cover and practice, practice, practice. The more they say the words—especially if they use their friends and classmates as an audience—the more natural the actual speech will sound. This kind of practice should also help reduce their level of anxiety.

- *Why can't I just speak off the top of my head? I hate speeches that sound "canned."*
  Answer: Like any piece of good writing, a strong speech relies heavily on pre-planning. The text does not suggest that students should write out a speech, memorize it, and then deliver to their audience. It does, however, advocate a six-step process of preparation. Illustrate for your students how even a minimal amount of planning can improve their speaking skills.

b. Writing Reflection
Leave a few minutes at the end of class for students to complete the Personal Journal section on page 204.

PREVIEW FOR NEXT CLASS
Ask students to get into groups of 2-3 and do the exercise on "Working Together" on page 222 prior to the next class meeting.

E. Test Questions

Multiple Choice - choose ONE answer per question.

1. According to your text, writing serves two purposes, exemplified in the terms _____ writing and _____ writing.
   a. communicative; descriptive
   b. creative; scientific
   c. exploratory; explanatory
   d. creative; concrete

2. Many writing experts believe that the writing step that should take the longest is
   a. prewriting or rehearsing.
   b. writing or drafting.
   c. rewriting or revision.
   d. none of these, all steps should be given the same amount of time.

3. This is when exploratory writing becomes a rough explanatory draft.
   a. Rewriting or revision
   b. Writing or drafting
   c. Prewriting or rehearsing
   d. None of the above

4. What's the first thing you should do when planning a successful speech?
   a. Prepare your notes
   b. Analyze your audience
   c. Organize your information
   d. Clarify your objective.

5. When visual aids are added to a presentation, listeners
   a. can absorb and recall more information.
   b. tend to become distracted and tune out.
   c. rate the presenter as more knowledgeable.
   d. view the presenter as cold and distant.

6. According to the text, a writer should spend _____ percent on the pre writing (including research and rumination) stage.
   a. 55
   b. 65
   c. 75
   d. 85

7. Which is NOT one of the six steps to successful speaking?
   a. Analyze your information
   b. Organize your information
   c. Prepare your notes
   d. Practice your delivery

8. To ensure that your main idea works in your speech, use the following supporting materials:
   a. examples.
   b. statistics.
   c. testimony.
   d. all of the above.

9. According to the text, a writer should spend _____percent of his time on the writing (first draft) stage.
   a. 10
   b. 5
   c. 1
   d. none of the above

10. When using notes to give a speech, the best speaking aid is a
    a. minimal outline.
    b. detailed outline.
    c. sketchy outline.
    d. none of the above

True/False

11. Prewriting is the explanatory part of the writing process.

12. Prewriting should take the shortest amount of time.

13. It's bad form to conclude a speech by saying "So in conclusion…"

14. While speaking to an audience, it is best not to make eye contact, as it can be distracting to both you and the listener.

15. Statistics are widely used as evidence in speeches.

Short Answer

16. What are the three stages of writing? Give your answer in the order of which step you spend the least time on to the one you spend the most time on.

17. Name the three most widely used forms of supporting materials.

18. List three ways you can practice your delivery.

19. List five questions to ask yourself when analyzing your audience.

20. What are three guidelines to follow as you select your visuals for a speech?

Essay

21. Define the difference between exploratory writing and explanatory writing and tell why it is important to go through one stage before moving to the other.

22. Imagine that your instructor assigns a 10-minute speech on a topic of your choice. Choose your topic, identify the six steps to success discussed in this chapter, and write about how you would complete each step in order to create the best presentation possible.

23. What was the most important lesson you learned from this chapter? Why is this so?

24. What are the advantages and disadvantages to using visual aids (mentioned on p. 193) in a speech. Do certain types of speeches require certain types of visuals? If so, why?

25. What behaviors are you planning to change after reading this chapter? Why?

CHAPTER 10 ANSWER KEY

1. c, p. 187
2. a, p. 188
3. b, p. 188
4. d, p. 192
5. a, p. 193
6. d, p. 190
7. a, p. 192
8. d, p. 198
9. c, p. 190
10. a, p. 194
11. false, p.188
12. false, p. 188
13. true, p.199
14. false, p.195
15. true, p.198

F. Web Resources

Prewriting Exercises – http://students.faulkner.edu/cwalker/Comp1/prewriting_exercises.htm
Most college students don't take the time to complete any prewriting exercises. Direct them to this site, which offers some quick but valuable prewriting exercises your students can employ on their next papers.

Revising Your Paper for Content – http://alpha.furman.edu/~moakes/Powerwrite/revise.htm

For some college students, revising means running spell check. This page debunks that myth and explains how students can revise their papers to improve content. It also contains a link to a section that does deal with revising for mechanics.

Great American Speeches – http://www.pbs.org/greatspeeches/
This rich resource affiliated with PBS not only contains speech texts, it also offers background information on each speaker, as well as several audio and video links. This site would be useful if you're planning on trying out Lecture Launcher 1.

Conquer Public Speaking Fear – http://www.stresscure.com/jobstress/speak.html
Best-selling author Dr. Morton C. Orman offers 11 principles to overcoming the fear of public speaking on this inspiring site.

Student Journal Writing – http://www.ericfacility.net/databases/ERIC_Digests/ed378587.html
This report, compiled by the Educational Resources Information Center (ERIC), lists different styles of student journals and discusses the effectiveness of each. It's particularly useful to instructors who have never incorporated journaling into their coursework.

AmeriCorps – http://www.americorps.org/
The homepage for AmeriCorps, one of the highest-profile networks of national service programs, boasts testimonials, research reports, and information on how to join and/or create new programs.

Public Speaking - http://www.selfgrowth.com/public.html, http://www.school-for-champions.com/speaking/resources.htm

G. For More Information

Carnegie, Dale. (1990). *The quick and easy way to effective speaking.* New York: Pocket Books.

Esposito, Janet E. (2000). *In the spotlight: Overcome your fear of public speaking and performing.* Southington, CT: Strong Books.

Finkelstein, Ellen. (2002). *How to do everything with PowerPoint.* New York: McGraw-Hill.

King, Stephen. (2000). *On writing.* New York: Scribner.

Mallon, Thomas. (2001). *Stolen words.* New York: Harcourt.

Chapter 11: Research and College Libraries

Ideas for Instruction and Instructor Training	Videos and CD-ROMs	Media Resources for Instructors	Media Resources for Students
Instructor's Manual (IM) Includes a brief lesson plan for Chapter 11, chapter objectives, lecture launchers, commentary on exercises in the book, and case studies. **Test Bank (in IM)** Multiple Choice, True/False, Short Answer and Essay Questions. Also available in ExamView® electronic format, which can be customized to fit your needs.	**ExamView® CD-ROM** Computerized version of the Test Bank items for Chapter 11.	**JOININ™** Hand-held audience response device allows students immediate response to multiple-choice questions, polls, and interactive exercises. **Multimedia Manager 2007 CD-ROM** PowerPoint presentations, video clips, images, and web links help with assembly, editing, and presentation of multimedia lectures.	**iLrn® Pin-Coded Website** Contains self-assessments, electronic journals that encourage students to reflect on their progress, essay questions and exercises, and Test Your Knowledge interactive quizzes for chapter 11. **InfoTrac® College Edition** May be bundled with text. *Keywords:* college success, liberal arts, goal setting, values, colleges, universities. **WebTutor™ Toolbox** Online course management tool for WebCT™ or Blackboard preloaded with text-specific content and media resources for Chapter 11.

A. Chapter Objectives

1. To help students understand how information is organized
2. To illustrate what membership and participation in the Information Society requires
3. To demonstrate the link between computer skills and success in any major or career
4. To teach students how to focus on a topic, narrow it, and shape it
5. To encourage students to experiment with a variety of search strategies and to use a wide range of information resources
6. To offer suggestions on the most effective avenues for getting help
7. To underscore the impact computer-related ethical and legal issues have on student's lives during and after college

B. Timing of Chapter Coverage

While it is important to get your students acquainted with the library as a campus resource early in the term, it will probably be more useful if you wait to cover the content of this chapter until later. Consider introducing your students to the physical layout and major service points of the library through a tour or an easy class activity. Making use of an information "scavenger hunt" can be a creative way to get your students to explore library resources.

Keep in mind that library and information resources can always be linked to discussions or projects in almost all the other chapters. Library research is more interesting and more relevant to students if library assignments are related to something from class. For example, as your class works through the time management chapter, ask if any of your students have projects in their other classes that will require them to use the library. This may help you decide when to teach this chapter. Be sure to share any assignments requiring library research with the librarians in advance. They'll be better able to help your students if they understand your own goals and objectives for assignments and can then offer advice and ideas for effective library assignments.

C. About This Chapter

First and foremost, do not hesitate to ask librarians for assistance when preparing for this chapter. If you are new to your campus or unfamiliar with some of the resources your students will be using, make sure you make time to get your own library orientation. Chances are the library and its resources have changed some from last year, let alone when you were in college. If your library doesn't have enough staff to provide tours or instructional sessions, familiarize yourself with new products, policies, and procedures on a regular basis.

Schedule time (during class or as an out-of-class assignment) for the students to tour the library. Prepare your class for selecting research topics and guide them in finding the right question or topic to research, making sure that it is not too narrow or too broad to adequately research.Think about having students work in groups. If your library doesn't offer tours, assign particular departments and services to a group of students and have them report back to the whole class. Pair students up to work through some of the exercises. They may be more likely to try different approaches and evaluate the information they find.

Talk to your librarians about ways you can incorporate information-seeking and evaluating skills into your course. Consider several smaller assignments instead of the typical term paper.

D. Suggested Outline for Addressing Topics in Chapter 11

STEP I: BEGIN WITH A LECTURE LAUNCHER OR ICEBREAKER ACTIVITY
STEP II: EMPLOY A VARIETY OF CLASSROOM ACTIVITIES
    a. Use the PowerPoint presentation from *Multimedia Manager 2007* resource
    b. Expand on key lesson themes
    c. Involve peer leaders
    d. Use chapter exercises
    e. Engage students in learning through case studies
STEP III: REVIEW & PREVIEW
    a. Address common questions and concerns about the topic
    b. Writing reflection
    c. Prepare for next class

Expanded Lesson Plan
STEP I: Lecture Launchers and Icebreakers

- Using either a hypothetical assignment or one your students are to complete, begin by asking them for ideas for a topic. Then as a group ask them to specify and narrow the topic. Once the topic is sufficiently focused, discuss ways for them to research the topic. If you've planned a library orientation, you can carry this example throughout that visit. Or, if you've scheduled time in a computer lab, you can show your students your school's online resources, how to conduct informed Internet searches, etc.

- To begin your discussion about plagiarism and its ramifications, consider discussing high-profile cases of professionals caught plagiarizing. Films for the Humanities and Sciences offers a video called *The Jayson Blair Story: Favoritism and Plagiarism at The New York Times* (http://www.films.com/Films_Home/Item.cfm/1/32499). Consider screening this film or another like it to open up a dialogue with your students about plagiarism and its consequences.

STEP II: Classroom Activities

a. Use the PowerPoint presentations in *Multimedia Manager 2007* resource to complement your mini lecture.

b. Key Teaching Themes

- **Search Engines**

  1. Break your students into small groups and assign them all the same topic.
  2. Have each group evaluate different search engines and other tools for finding information on the web by using their assigned topic. This way they can learn the ins and outs of at least one search engine.
  3. Have each group make a presentation to the rest of the class on the special features of the search engine, and what information they found on the shared topic.
  4. Besides reading the help screens of the search engine, suggest your students consult "Search Engine Watch" http://searchenginewatch.com/. "Search Engine Watch" is a convenient way to keep up with developments and includes searching tips as well as ratings and reviews of search engines.

- **Professional Values**

  1. Combine investigating a possible profession (Exercise 11.3) with the idea of professional values by having your students write about an ethical problem faced by those in their chosen profession.
  2. As a starting point, your students might want to consult the following reference books: *Encyclopedia of Ethics*, *Encyclopedia of Applied Ethics*, and *Encyclopedia of Bioethics*.

3. Have your students identify a major association for the profession and see if they have a code of ethics. Good sources include *Codes of Professional Responsibility, Professional Ethics and Insignia,* and association web sites.
4. You could have your students write a reaction paper or build a case study based on an article they find about an ethical problem.

c. Group Activities (see b above)

d. Peer Leader Assistance

Organization is key to successfully implementing this topic. There will be many logistical concerns, from making reservations for a library tour to inviting guest speakers. Involve your peer leader in all aspects of the planning.

e. Case Studies

Pat

Pat's local newspaper publishes an ad for what appears to be a terrific job with a company that Pat would really like to work with. Pat interviews with the company and takes the offered position. Within six months, to Pat's surprise and dismay, the company closes its doors leaving Pat without a job. As it turns out, the company had been in financial trouble for some time.

Discussion Questions:
1. What does this scenario say about the power of information?
2. Who held the power in this case?
3. Was it ethical for the company not to alert Pat to the financial problems during the interview?
4. Does Pat have any responsibility for being out of a job? What could Pat have done?

Jordan

Jordan's composition instructor has assigned the class a research paper that focuses on a controversial topic of the students' choice. In his senior year of high school, Jordan wrote a paper about the ethics of psychosurgery and received an "A." To save time, Jordan figures he will beef up this paper for his composition instructor. However, his composition instructor has required students to use MLA style for their papers. Jordan's original paper used APA style, and in revamping the paper he forgets to change the citations to MLA. He turns in the "new" paper and is surprised when his instructor calls him into her office to ask him if he has plagiarized portions of his project.

Discussion Questions:
1. Does Jordan's actions constitute plagiarism? Why or why not?
2. If you were Jordan, how would you justify using the old paper?
3. If you were Jordan's instructor, what actions would you take?

f. Chapter Exercises

- **Exercise 11.1: Getting Comfortable in Your Library**
  This exercise could be completed during a library orientation session or you could assign it   for homework. Consider creating a scavenger hunt within the library setting and having your students complete it in pairs or small groups.

- **Exercise 11.2: Getting Oriented to Periodicals**
  Again, this exercise is well suited for a library orientation session. If your library does not offer such sessions, consider leading your students through one yourself.

- **Exercise 11.3: Looking Up a Career**
  Assign this activity out of class and have your students write about what they found, either in their journals or a separate report.

STEP III: Review and Preview

REVIEW

a. Address Common Questions and Concerns of First-Year Students:

- *Why do I have to do this? I already know how to use a library.*
  Answer: College libraries have vast resources with which students may not be familiar. In addition to getting them acquainted with the physical layout of the library, it's important to spend time introducing them to any electronic resources specific to your school and/or course. While many of your students may feel comfortable using web-based resources, not all may have extensive experience working in this medium.

- *How can I ask for help without looking stupid?*
  Answer: Librarians are information experts trained to assist and guide your students to get the resources they need. They are more than happy to help your students, and do not find any question "silly" or "stupid." If possible, have one of the reference librarians at your school come and speak to your class or help conduct a library orientation center. Sometimes, meeting a librarian face-to-face in this type of setting is enough to make your students feel at ease in terms of asking for support.

- *Everything I need is on the web. Why do I need to use other types of sources?*
  Answer: A well-researched paper draws its sources across all media – books, magazines, academic journals, the Internet. While the web provides a vast amount of material right at the students' fingertips, it's important for them to learn the "old-fashioned" methods of research as well. If you assign them a research paper, consider putting restrictions on the type of sources they can use. For instance, if you require six sources, tell students that four of the six must not be Internet sources, and that one must be an academic journal. This will force your students to seek information from other places.

- *Why do I have to write down all this information on each source?*
  Answer: Any time you use someone else's published words or ideas, you must give these sources proper credit. Failing to do so constitutes plagiarism. Most colleges consider plagiarism a form of cheating, and committing plagiarism carries serious consequences. To help students avoid plagiarizing their sources—even accidentally—it's vital that you impress upon them the importance of taking good notes and keeping bibliographical information organized.

- *My teachers can't possibly keep up with all of the web sites that sell papers and I have four due in one week. Nobody's going to know if I borrow just one from the Internet. It's not a big deal, is it?*
  Answer: When you are doing a unit on plagiarism, and what constitutes plagiarism, it's a good idea to talk to students about the growing number of Internet sites that can track papers purchased on the web. Illustrate, too, how running a simple Google search can turn up most plagiarized passages as well. It's crucial that your students are aware that while technology may help them cheat, it also helps you identify instances of cheating. Also, if for some reason you haven't gone over your school's policies on academic honest, cheating, and plagiarism, now is an excellent time to do so. Impress upon your students that any cheating, intentional or otherwise, could lead to failure of an assignment or course, or, depending on how strict policies are, expulsion.

b. Writing Reflection

- Choose one or more of the reflection questions on page 224 in the text and ask students to respond in writing.

PREVIEW FOR NEXT CLASS
Decide whether you want students to complete a career inventory test (see exercise 12.2) before the next class and inform them accordingly.

E. Test Questions

Multiple Choice - choose ONE answer per question.

1. According to the text, _____are the world's leading authorities on how to find information.
   a. the information professionals at your library
   b. the American workforce
   c. the GNP
   d. knowledge and research

2. Galloping New Ignorance (GNI) refers to
   a. the assumption that the huge amounts of manageable information available at the press of a button confer knowledge.

    b. the knowledge that electronic information is not the gospel—that most electronic information should be ignored in favor of information appearing in print.

    c. the growing tendency students have to steal information from the Internet instead of searching for information that will help them learn independently.

    d. none of the above.

3. Analytical information provides
    a. basic and elementary material.
    b. descriptive details about a topic.
    c. data about origins, behaviors, differences, and uses.
    d. rigorously researched documentation.

4. Cultural Literacy refers to
    a. knowing how to use electronic methods for constructing presentations of what you have found and analyzed.
    b. having facility with various formats—film, tape, CDs—and the machines that operate them.
    c. being comfortable with people from different backgrounds and belief systems.
    d. knowing what has gone on and is going on around you.

5. The only time it's okay NOT to cite information is
    a. when you use someone else's words.
    b. when you summarize someone else's ideas.
    c. when you combine two or three people's words and ideas into your own sentence.
    d. when you are writing something original that doesn't rely on source material.

6. It is safe to say that we live in an _____ Age.
    a. Agricultural
    b. Information
    c. AEC
    d. All of the above

7. Galloping New Ignorance (GNI) is so commonplace that it infects
    a. smart people.
    b. decision makers.
    c. a and b
    d. none of the above

8. _____ information supplies data about origins, behaviors, differences, and uses
    a. Analytical
    b. Definitional
    c. Original
    d. none of the above

9. Knowing what has gone on and is going on around you is called
   a. computer literacy.
   b. media literacy.
   c. cultural literacy.
   d. none of the above

10. _____ information neither assumes nor requires prior knowledge about the topic
   a. Introductory
   b. Definitional
   c. Analytical
   d. all of the above

True/False

11. Since there is nothing wrong with a magazine pushing a personal agenda, it's not important for a student to be aware of their editorial biases.

12. An index is different from a catalog.

13. A scholarly journal often contains articles reviewed by the author's peers in the field.

14. It's best not to approach a librarian for help until you've already gotten a good deal of the foundation research completed.

15. If you accidentally commit plagiarism, the odds are that your professors will understand.

Short Answer

16. Name the three types of information literacy your text discusses, as well as their definitions.

17. Give an example of a topic, an inquiry task, and a product. Explain the differences between each.

18. List at least four differences between scholarly journals and popular magazines.

19. In learning to be information literate, what four things do you need to remember about information and why?

20. Explain the difference between *subject* searches and *keyword* searches.

Essay

21. No doubt you've heard our time characterized as "The Information Age." How do you define information?

22. T.S. Eliot wrote, "Where is the wisdom we have lost in knowledge? Where is the knowledge we have lost in information?" Do you think T.S. Eliot would have coined the term, the Information Age? How is information different from knowledge and wisdom?

23. Describe some of your experiences on the Web. Which search engines and types of searches have worked best for you? Why?

24. Did you learn anything new about search engines and databases in this chapter that you think will be helpful in the future? If so, what? Also, have you been aware of variations in the validity of web sites and the information they contain? What things will you now pay closer attention to as you visit various web sites?

25. What behaviors are you planning to change after reading this chapter? Why?

CHAPTER 11 ANSWER KEY

1. a, p. 208
2. a, p. 209
3. c, p. 211
4. d, p. 211
5. d, p. 219
6. b, p. 208
7. c, p. 209
8. a, p. 211
9. c, p. 211
10. a, p. 211
11. false, pp. 214-215
12. true, p. 217
13. false, p. 217
14. false, p. 219
15. Computer, media, and cultural (definitions will vary), p. 211
16. Answers will vary, p. 213
17. Answers will vary, p. 217
18. Answers will vary
19. Answers will vary
20. Answers will vary

F. Web Resources

Information Literacy – http://bulldogs.tlu.edu/mdibble/doril/
This page contains a directory of online resources pertaining to information literacy.

Researching a Topic http://www.dartmouth.edu/~writing/materials/about.shtml
The Composition Center at Dartmouth College offers some great resources for your students. In addition to information on finding sources, the site contains strategies for using those sources—everything from summarizing and organizing them to citing them proper

Plagiarism.org – http://www.plagiarism.org/
This site, geared toward students and educators, deals with Internet plagiarism, how to identify it, and how to combat it. This site makes an excellent companion to Lecture Launcher 2.

EasyBib.com – http://www.easybib.com/
This site offers a free feature which helps students create MLA-style entries for a works cited list. Students needing to use the APA format can access a converter for a small fee.

National Forum on Information Literacy – http://www.infolit.org/
The NFIL, based at San Jose State University, has written several reports and conducted numerous programs focusing on the importance of information literacy. You can access them on their site. In addition, this web page features definitions of different kinds of literacy (more extensive than the one found in the text) and a list of links dealing with the issues information literacy raises.

TurnItIn.com – http://www.turnitin.com/
The web's most powerful plagiarism deterrent, TurnItIn.com lets instructors check the originality of student papers. It also offers instructors a system for grading papers online, keeping track of grades, and creating an online portfolio of student work.

These sites contain online handouts that will help in the writing process:
http://owl.english.purdue.edu/handouts/index.html, http://www.wecc.rpi.edu/.

G. For More Information

Burkhardt, Joanna M. et al. (2003). *Teaching information literacy: 35 practical, standards-based exercises for college students.* Chicago, IL: American Library Association Editions.

Gibaldi, Joseph and Phyllis Franken. (2003). *MLA handbook for writers of research papers (6th ed).* New York: Modern Language Association of America.

Harris, Robert A. (2001). *The plagiarism handbook: Strategies for preventing, detecting, and dealing with plagiarism.* Los Angeles, CA: Pyrczak Pub.

Mann, Thomas. (1998). *The Oxford guide to library research.* London: Oxford University Press.

Sherman, Chris and Gary Price. (2001). *The invisible web: Uncovering information sources search engines can't see.* Chicago, IL: Independent Publishers Group.

Chapter 12: Majors and Careers—Making the Right Choices

Ideas for Instruction and Instructor Training	Videos and CD-ROMs	Media Resources for Instructors	Media Resources for Students
Instructor's Manual (IM) Includes a brief lesson plan for Chapter 12, chapter objectives, lecture launchers, commentary on exercises in the book, and case studies. **Test Bank (in IM)** Multiple Choice, True/False, Short Answer and Essay Questions. Also available in ExamView® electronic format, which can be customized to fit your needs.	*10 Things Every Student Needs to Succeed in College* **Video** 6-minute segment entitled "Explore Your Career Options." **ExamView® CD-ROM** Computerized version of the Test Bank items for Chapter 12.	**JOININ™** Hand-held audience response device allows students immediate response to multiple-choice questions, polls, and interactive exercises. **Multimedia Manager 2007 CD-ROM** PowerPoint presentations, video clips, images, and web links help with assembly, editing, and presentation of multimedia lectures.	**iLrn® Pin-Coded Website** Contains self-assessments, electronic journals that encourage students to reflect on their progress, essay questions and exercises, and Test Your Knowledge interactive quizzes for chapter 12. **InfoTrac® College Edition** May be bundled with text. *Keywords:* college success, liberal arts, goal setting, values, colleges, universities. **WebTutor™ Toolbox** Online course management tool for WebCT™ or Blackboard preloaded with text-specific content and media resources for Chapter 12.

A. Chapter Objectives

1. To illustrate how majors and careers both are and aren't linked
2. To introduce a timely process of career planning and the selection of a major
3. To understand the dynamics and demands of the 21st century workplace
4. To identify resources that can assist students through the career planning process
5. To engage in building tools necessary for finding employment

B. Timing of Chapter Coverage

The introduction of career-decision making material could be addressed in the middle of the term. By then, students have had time to adjust to their new environments and are getting acclimated to college classes and exams. Shortly after midterms, students often express doubt as to why they are in college. This is a good time for them to sort out their interests and reaffirm their educational pursuits. This does not mean that they have to declare a major or have a specific career in mind when the course is over. However, they should have a better sense of who they are and what classes may be of interest to them.

C. About This Chapter

Goal setting in general, and career planning in particular, are real problem areas for students, especially first-year students. Probably only a minority of your students are self-disciplined enough to engage in rigorous career planning. Others are simply not mentally ready to undertake career planning. Still others, especially the older student, are so sure of the choices they've already made that they will regard any time you spend on career planning as a waste of their time.

Therefore, at best, you can expect your students to understand the process of career planning by the end of this chapter. They should know the major steps of the process, how to perform them, and what resources exist on your campus to help them as they move along the path of goal setting and career planning. This seemingly "modest" achievement is really very important in that it lets the students know that there is a process they can follow, and informs them of who can help them when they are ready. It is also another way of demonstrating your concern for them.

Before beginning this section, you should decide how much time you want to devote to it. Assess where your students' attitudes and motivation for career planning lie and then decide on how much and what you will cover from this chapter. Use some of the Lecture Launchers or chapter exercises to stimulate interest before you teach the chapter. Depending on your students' attitudes toward career planning, you might decide to spend time on other activities.

D. Suggested Outline for Addressing Topics in Chapter 12

> **STEP I:** BEGIN WITH A LECTURE LAUNCHER OR ICEBREAKER ACTIVITY
> **STEP II:** EMPLOY A VARIETY OF CLASSROOM ACTIVITIES
>
>   a. Use PowerPoint presentation from ***Multimedia Manager 2007*** resource
>   b. Expand on key lesson themes
>   c. Involve peer leaders
>   d. Use chapter exercises
>   e. Engage students in learning through case studies
>
> **STEP III:** REVIEW & PREVIEW
>
>   a. Address common questions and concerns about the topic
>   b. Writing reflection
>   c. Prepare for next class

Expanded Lesson Plan

STEP I: Lecture Launchers and Icebreakers

- Today's students can not only choose their careers, but they will be able to change their careers later in life if they so desire. Encourage students to think about members of their families and the attitudes they have toward their work. Try to end the discussion by having them recognize that they have choices. After this discussion, ask your students to submit at least two questions about career choices. Specifically, what do they want to learn from the chapter? You might then compile these questions in a list and distribute them to the whole class to be used as a guide to the chapter. These questions will also be a guide to you as you teach the unit.

- Begin class by reading excerpts from *Working* by Studs Terkel. These excerpts will illustrate that some workers are very happy with the work they do, whereas others (perhaps the majority) are terribly unhappy with their work. This can open up a discussion where your students explore their notions about work and the kinds of satisfaction they expect to get from their future jobs. Is a job just a way to make a living? Is happiness in a job important? Must a job provide satisfactions beyond the paycheck or job security? In conducting this discussion (and others), don't be afraid to cite your own experiences, but do avoid being preachy. Be sure to capitalize on the nontraditional students in your class. They can be a treasure trove of experience.

- Depending on your class, it may be of value to share some of your career development experiences. Think back to your first year. Did you begin college knowing what career you wanted? If so, did you stick to that decision? Were you uncomfortable with that inevitable question, "What's your major?" Did you think that you were alone in feeling clueless about your future? Encourage your students to share their career goals (or lack of goals) with each other. This will help them realize that many of their fellow students are as undecided as they are. You want to let them know that being undecided is okay. Teaching career planning is also a way of letting first-year students know that there are sources that can help them make decisions.

STEP II: Classroom Activities

a. Use the PowerPoint presentations in *Multimedia Manager 2007* to complement your mini lecture.

b. Key Teaching Themes

- **The New Economy**
  Address points in the section on Careers and New Economy on pages 229-232. Use the "pointers" in the margins of these pages to emphasize this section.

- **Choosing Courses**
  Choosing courses and faculty is something that an academic advisor may assist students with. However, there are other sources of information that students can use to make these important decisions. Place students in small groups to generate ideas for alternate sources of information that will be of use to them as they choose courses and faculty. Such sources of information might include the college catalog or bulletin; departmental course descriptions; course syllabi (obtained from other students, academic department offices, or

directly from faculty); required textbooks (can be viewed at the college bookstore); faculty members (other than official academic advisors); and other students' recommendations.

- **Career Counselor/Center Visit**
  To make students aware of campus resources and how they can use them. Either invite your campus career counselor to class, or plan a class trip to the counseling center. In either case, the career counselor can provide an authoritative summary of what you have already taught. Consider having the career counselor look at some students' resumes, possibly critiquing them in the classroom setting (you can have the counselor remove the students' names and addresses from the tops of the resumes to protect the students' privacy). Ask the counselor to distribute literature about the counseling center and all of the resources available to your students. This is a good way of demonstrating the commitment of your campus to the students' ultimate success. Whether or not you choose to invite the career counselor to class, at the close of this unit your students will have identified, articulated, and started to integrate their interests, current skills, aptitudes, personality characteristics, and values.

c. Group Activities

- Have teams of students generate a list of academic or personal problems they might need help with. Arrange the problems into categories and identify campus resources that can offer help.

- Have students jot down five things they find interesting. Collect responses and form small "interest groups" by students who listed similar things. Have each group identify what kinds of careers their interests might be useful for. Or, form four-member teams with the same academic major or students who share similar career interests. One pair of students within each team might research internship opportunities while the other pair investigates related service learning opportunities. The group's final product would represent a composite of available "experiential learning" opportunities tied to their majors, interests, skills, etc.

d. Peer Leader Assistance

- Consider inviting a recent graduate of your institution into the classroom to discuss his or her experiences in searching for a major and related career. This could be a graduate who had trouble choosing a major or who has had more than one career. You could also arrange for a small panel of several seniors who can discuss how they went about making their decisions about courses and careers.

e. Case Studies

Andrew
For as long as he could remember, Andrew had wanted to be a physician. So when he entered college, he majored in science as preparation for medical school. But although he

155

earned good grades in his science courses, he found that he was bored with science in general. He made an appointment with his adviser and told him of his feelings. His advisor said, "Andrew, I know what you mean. Lots of people go through this stage. But your grades are so good that I'm going to urge you to continue. Then, when you begin medical school, you can decide whether or not you want to stay there. If you don't, your education will have prepared you for a number of other careers, so what have you got to lose?" Andrew left the office feeling confused. "If I don't enjoy something," he said, "why should I keep on doing it?"

Discussion Questions:
1. What's your opinion of the advice the advisor gave Andrew?
2. Physicians make good money. Is this a strong reason for Andrew to stick to his plans? Explain your answer.
3. How might a visit to the career center provide Andrew with some insight into his dilemma?
4. Andrew is getting a solid liberal arts education anyway. What's he really got to lose by staying on track for the present?

Becca
Becca came to college and took classes for a year and a half. Not knowing what she wanted to major in, she didn't do that well in her classes. So, she decided to take a year off from college and work. Becca has been working as a bookkeeper for a printing company for one semester now. While she likes making money, she is still not satisfied and thinks that going back to college may be a good idea for her. However, she still has no clue of what career or major to choose. Becca is apprehensive about going back to college because she is so undecided.

Discussion Questions:
1. What is Becca's dilemma?
2. What suggestions could you give Becca?
3. What issues should Becca address before deciding whether or not to go back to school?
4. How can Becca come to a decision about college and work?
5. Where can Becca go for help?

f. Chapter Exercises

- ### Exercise 12.1: What Are Your Life Goals?
  Choosing a career starts with identifying goals. Have students complete this exercise individually in class. They can share their rankings in pairs or groups. Encourage them to share their reasoning behind their choices.

- ### Exercise 12.2: Finding Your Interests
  Part A of this exercise can be completed individually or directed by you in a group setting. Part B could become part of a larger assignment, such as a 3-5 page paper.

- **Exercise 12.3: Using Your Career Library**
  Again, this is an exercise that students will need to complete out of class.

- **Exercise 12.4: Investigating an Occupation**
  This exercise can be completed out of class. You may also want to have them record their reaction to the experience.

- **Exercise 12.5: Writing a Resume and Cover Letter**
  If you're only going to assign your students one exercise from this chapter, this is the one. Even first-year students may be preparing to explore internship opportunities, and knowing how to create a resume and craft a strong cover letter are some of the more practical skills they can glean from this section.

- **Exercise 12.4: Investigating an Occupation**
  This exercise can also be completed out of class.

STEP III: Review and Preview

REVIEW

a. Address Common Questions and Concerns of First-Year Students:

- *I'm only a first-year student. Why should I be concerned with careers now?*
  Answer: Many students will not see the need for exploring majors or careers so early in their education. Explain to them that selecting a major and career is a process that involves self-knowledge and takes time. Encourage them to begin this process right away so that when the time comes for a decision, they will be prepared.

- *If it's true that my generation will change careers five times, why is career planning so important?*
  Answer: It is true that the workplace has changed dramatically for employees and that nowadays people make multiple career changes. Emphasize to students that the decisions they make in college will impact where they end up in the workplace. Encourage them to find different ways to use their majors for employment and to undertake a thorough career-planning program.

- *I already know what I want to do. Why do I have to go through all this boring stuff?*
  Answer: While some students will have a strong sense of their career, today's work world is constantly changing and will require that they come well prepared and with the understanding that there are no guarantees of ongoing employment. They stand to change jobs more than ever. Explain to students that they must explore and identify their interests, values, goals, personality type, and aptitudes, and accurately link them to possible careers.

- *How do I know I will have the skills and competencies I need when I graduate?*
  Answer: The responsibility for knowing what skills are needed for various professions falls on the student. The last thing they want to do is graduate from college and find out that they are missing a skill, competency, or certification that is critical for employment in a particular field. Emphasize that we are all responsible for our careers. Students can do research to find out what skills and competencies are needed for the fields they have chosen.

- *If I'm not signed up for accounting first term, can I still major in business (or any similar curriculum-related question)?*
  Answer: Sometimes first-year students think that if they are not registered for a particular class required for a major during the first term or year, it means they cannot select that discipline as a major. They may see their friends or roommate starting off with a class in their major and begin to worry. Assure them that there will be time to "catch up" on taking classes required for certain majors as they explore different careers. However, encourage students to systematically explore and plan if they are undecided about their major. Warn them of the danger of taking random courses for too long and accumulating excess credits that may not meet the requirements for the major they finally decide on.

b. Writing Reflection

- Have students complete the questions on page 251.

PREVIEW FOR NEXT CLASS
Ask students to complete Exercise 13.2 and bring it to the next class.

E. Test Questions

Multiple Choice - choose ONE answer per question.

1. As a result of workforce restructuring wrought by the New Economy, major changes have taken place in
   a. how we work.
   b. where we work.
   c. the ways we prepare students for the world of work.
   d. all of the above

2. To advance your career, you must
   a. accept the risks that accompany employment.
   b. plan for the future.
   c. a & b
   d. none of the above

3. According to John Holland, for someone in the _____ category, accounting would be an ideal occupation.
   a. realistic
   b. social
   c. investigative
   d. conventional

4. According to John Holland, for someone in the _____ category, marine science would be an ideal occupation.
   a. realistic
   b. social
   c. investigative
   d. conventional

5. When writing a resume, you should
   a. aim for it to be one page in length.
   b. place your hobbies and interests high up to make yourself appear more well-rounded.
   c. list a minimum of five personal and professional references.
   d. print it out on bright paper to distinguish you from the other applicants.

6. The process of making a career choice begins with
   a. understanding your values and motivations.
   b. identifying your interests.
   c. a & b
   d. none of the above

7. A good career plan should eventually include
   a. building on your strengths and developing your weaker skills.
   b. writing a convincing resume and cover letter.
   c. a & b
   d. none of the above

8. Service learning allows you to
   a. apply academic theories and ideas to actual practice.
   b. make your hobbies and interests a high priority.
   c. earn extra money.
   d. all of the above

9. According to the text, two types of skills are essential to employment and to life; they are
   a. content and transferable.
   b. mastery and interests.
   c. personal and professional.
   d. none of the above

10. You'll need a resume
    a. after you get your degree.
    b. before you finish high school.
    c. before you finish college.
    d. none of the above

True/False

11. A college degree does not guarantee employment.

12. Bringing work home on a regular basis is the sign of an effective employee.

13. Don't bother networking with anyone who can't directly help you achieve your goals.

14. Most occupational fields do not require a specific major.

15. You should choose your career based on future earnings.

Short Answer

16. Name the six general categories of people identified by John Holland.

17. List at least three factors affecting career choice.

18. What are four ways you can gain experience in a potential career?

19. List some four differences between content skills and transferable skills.

20. List four resources you can use in your search for an off-campus job.

Essay

21. How does the text define the economy of the early 21st century? As you are preparing to begin your career, what are some things you need to keep in mind to "survive the changing economy?"

22. Which of Holland's six categories do you best fall into? What are some careers that Holland predicts would appeal to you? Which one do you find yourself most interested in? How would you go about investigating the career?

23. If you have already identified a career that you wish to pursue, shadow someone for a day who is presently working in that field. Write an essay describing your activities for the day, why you wish to pursue this field, what strengths you presently possess that supports your desire to pursue this field, and what you still need to do to in order to qualify for a position in this field.

24. Describe the career you wish to have in ten years. Develop a cover letter and resume that would guarantee that you get this job.

25. Describe the career that you wish to have five in years. Interview someone who is presently working in this field. What academic preparation was required for this job? What challenges did the person encounter while preparing for this job and how did he/she address these issues?

CHAPTER 12 ANSWER KEY
1. c, p. 229
2. b, p. 230
3. d, p. 235
4. c, p. 235
5. a, p. 244
6. c, p 236
7. c, p. 237
8. a, p. 240
9. a, p.241
10. c, p. 244
11. true, p. 229
12. false, p. 228
13. false, p. 229
14. true, p. 229
15. false, p. 218
16. realistic, investigative, artistic, social, enterprising, conventional, p. 231
17. Three of the following: interests, skills, aptitudes, personality, life goals, and work values, pp. 237-239
18. Four of the following: volunteer/service learning, study abroad, internships and co-ops, on-campus employment, student projects/competitions, and research, pp. 239-230

F. Web Resources

Choosing a Major – http://www2.ucsc.edu/porter/choosing.html
This page debunks some of the myths about choosing a major, such as "Picking a major and a career are basically the same thing" and "The major I pick now will determine my lifelong career."

The Career Key – http://www.careerkey.org/english/. Direct your students to The Career Key, a free test that measures skills, abilities, values, interest, and personality. It also offers information about the jobs for which it identifies aptitude.

Resumes – http://jobsmart.org/tools/resume/index.cfm. A feature of JobStar Central, this page offers information about creating a resume, as well as samples of different resume formats. It includes a feature that can help students determine what kind of resume would work best for them.

Cover Letters – http://www.careerlab.com/letters/default.htm. From CareerLab, this page offers great strategies for writing various types of cover letters—everything from answering a want ad to sending the most appropriate thank you letter after an interview. Each article is accompanied by an extensive set of examples your students can use as models.

Career Planning - http://quintcareers.com/ is a career planning and job-hunting resource guide and http://www.careerbuilder.com is a comprehensive career planning website.

The Self-Directed Search – http://www.self-directed-search.com/
For around $10, your students can take the official John Holland Self-Directed Search assessment on this page. The test takes fifteen minutes and results include a list of occupations, fields of study, and even leisure activities well-suited to the taker's particular type.

What Can I Do with a Major In …? – http://www.uncwil.edu/stuaff/career/Majors/
The University of North Carolina at Wilmington offers this site, which will give your students an idea of what career paths their major will open up for them.

G. For More Information

Block, Jay A., et al. (1997). *101 best resumes: Endorsed by the professional association of resume writers.* New York: McGraw-Hill Trade.

Gordon, Virginia N., et al. (2000). *Academic advising: A comprehensive handbook.* San Francisco, CA: Jossey-Bass.

Lore, Nicholas. (1998). *The pathfinder: How to choose or change your career for a lifetime of satisfaction and success.* New York: Fireside.

MacHado, Julio, ed. (2002). *Fishing for a major.* New York: Natavi Guides, Inc.

Prince, Jeffrey P. and Lisa J. Heiser. (2000). *Essentials of career interest assessment.* San Francisco, CA: John Wiley & Sons.

Chapter 13: Relationships

Ideas for Instruction and Instructor Training	Videos and CD-ROMs	Media Resources for Instructors	Media Resources for Students
Instructor's Manual (IM) Includes a brief lesson plan for Chapter 13, chapter objectives, lecture launchers, commentary on exercises in the book, and case studies. **Test Bank (in IM)** Multiple Choice, True/False, Short Answer and Essay Questions. Also available in ExamView® electronic format, which can be customized to fit your needs.	***10 Things Every Student Needs to Succeed in College* Video** 6-minute segment entitled "Building Relationships." **ExamView® CD-ROM** Computerized version of the Test Bank items for Chapter 13.	**JOININ™** Hand-held audience response device allows students immediate response to multiple-choice questions, polls, and interactive exercises. **Multimedia Manager 2007 CD-ROM** PowerPoint presentations, video clips, images, and web links help with assembly, editing, and presentation of multimedia lectures.	**iLrn® Pin-Coded Website** Contains self-assessments, electronic journals that encourage students to reflect on their progress, essay questions and exercises, and Test Your Knowledge interactive quizzes for chapter 13. **InfoTrac® College Edition** May be bundled with text. *Keywords:* college success, liberal arts, goal setting, values, colleges, universities. **WebTutor™ Toolbox** Online course management tool for WebCT™ or Blackboard preloaded with text-specific content and media resources for Chapter 13.

A. Chapter Objectives

1. To explore different types of relationships and how they affect students
2. To determine whether a serious relationship is right for you
3. To add perspective to students' relationships with their parents
4. To reinforce the value of diversity and cultural understanding in relationships
5. To point out the kinds of relationships that should be off-limits

B. Timing of Chapter Coverage

This chapter can be covered any time in the term. You may be able to cover sections of it within the context of other chapters. Because relationships are very much on the minds of entering students from day one, you may choose to cover this chapter nearer to the beginning of the course. However, it is probably best to give your students a chance to become acquainted with one another before discussing some of the sensitive topics in this chapter. This information on relationships and diversity will work very well if you choose to teach it in conjunction with the chapter on values.

C. About This Chapter

A key to using this chapter successfully is your acknowledgment that the two-thirds or more of their waking hours that students spend on things other than their studies are indeed important, and are a vital part of the education they will receive and remember from their college years. We are struck by how much student energy goes into dating, as well as how much anxiety and pain often result. Students typically blame their dating and mating frustrations on the other person. It is important that they come to see the role of their own distorted perceptions, their own choices, and their own approaches in determining the outcomes of their relationships.

Much of the student dating game is sexually driven, and a surprising number of students, especially women, take the risks without actually preferring to engage in the sexual activity, and without even enjoying it to any great degree. Consideration of when sex is appropriate, and what the emotional outcomes should be, is therefore quite important.

Your class is likely to contain at least some homosexual students, and it is important to acknowledge their existence and special issues. Because homophobia is often high among entering students, this part of the chapter should be of concern to the whole class. A scientifically interesting treatment of homosexuality, well written and in layman's terms, appears as a chapter in Martin Seligman's book, *What You Can Change . . . and What You Can't*. (See "For More Information.") Good guest speakers are often available from gay/lesbian/bisexual groups on campus or in the community, and they are experienced at handling the questions that commonly come up. Students may be indignant and set in their beliefs about homosexuality due to their religion; yet to think of homosexuality not as a disorder or disease, but as a religious difference subject to our mutual freedom of religion, is usually new to freshmen. To let the discussion turn to arguing points of any particular religion, however, is to tread swiftly into a morass.

Traditional aged students may find their parents to be "impossible." A sensitivity to the parents' perspective needs to be encouraged. The frequency of genuinely dysfunctional family situations is significant, but relatively low; many frictions with parents stem from simpler misperceptions and misunderstandings that are more easily dealt with. The "empty nest syndrome" is mainly a myth, but major developmental changes are occurring in traditionally aged students as they evaluate and adjust their relationships to their parents.

If you're game for trying something unusual but very powerful, try contacting the traditional aged students' parents in connection with your special course for entering students. First, explain to the students what you have in mind and why, and **get their written permission**; virtually none will refuse, especially if you let them know you have some sense about what they wouldn't want shared with their parents, such as their love lives, their personal activities, etc.

Early in the semester, write each parent a letter, perhaps accompanied by a few course materials, introducing yourself and explaining the course. Parents are very interested in learning about one of the persons who is teaching their son or daughter and what is happening in one of their courses. Include a few comments about the student, so it will be clear that you already know him or her individually. Invite parents to contact you if they ever have a question or problem with the college or university. If you have time, follow up with a short phone call—the parents will be thrilled. At the end of the course, send another letter discussing the student's progress and if contact with campus resources is needed, parents can get help for them there. Thank them for investing in your institution and entrusting their son or daughter to it and to you. Be as upbeat and positive as possible.

The institutional goodwill this simple gesture generates is enormous. It is humanizing for us as teachers to remember that each traditional aged entering student represents the hopes and dreams of real, delightful people of our own generation. The rewards may even be more tangible: One of our entering student's parents was so touched by the parent contact program that he donated $10,000 to the university in appreciation for it. We would be happy to share detailed plans and materials with any instructors or institutions interested in trying this approach.

Statistically, residence hall living and involvement with campus organizations significantly increase the odds of academic survival and persistence. Many students will be commuters, but for those in residence halls, successful adjustment needs to be encouraged, and all students should make significant connection to at least one campus organization.

We are powerfully persuaded of the value of co-op programs and service learning for today's students. Trends in the area of service learning are particularly exciting, and you would be on sound empirical as well as philosophical ground to urge or require your students to participate in service learning. It is important for students to see service learning not only as something to do for others, but also something that will be of great value to themselves.

If you read student journals over the course of the semester, you will find them dealing again and again with relationships—sometimes with pleasure, but sometimes with significant frustration or pain. If you have chosen to cover this chapter early in the course, you can refer to points or material in it when you write comments in your students' journals. Students may seem remarkably shortsighted or unperceptive in dealing with their relationships. What may seem entirely obvious to you may literally not even have occurred to them. Don't hesitate to write comments to your students when this happens. You don't have to be a psychologist or counselor—just say what you would say if you popped on your mom, dad, or advisor hat. And if you think a student needs a professional counselor, don't hesitate to suggest it. Students rarely resent this, and most appreciate your concern, even if they don't take your advice. Students are deeply grateful for your role as a confidant and your feedback and attention to their social dilemmas.

We repeat: Learning to deal constructively with relationships is a genuinely educational part of your entering students' experience. You may be sure that your facilitation of their understanding and maturing in relationships will be an appropriate and welcome part of their college education.

D. Suggested Outline for Addressing Topics in Chapter 13

> **STEP I:** BEGIN WITH A LECTURE LAUNCHER OR ICEBREAKER ACTIVITY
> **STEP II:** EMPLOY A VARIETY OF CLASSROOM ACTIVITIES
>   a. Use PowerPoint presentation from *Multimedia Manager 2007* resource
>   b. Expand on key lesson themes
>   c. Involve peer leaders
>   d. Use chapter exercises
>   e. Engage students in learning through case studies
> **STEP III:** REVIEW & PREVIEW
>   a. Address common questions and concerns about the topic
>   b. Writing reflection
>   c. Prepare for next class

Expanded Lesson Plan

STEP I: Lecture Launchers and Icebreakers

- Consider each of the following "axioms of relationships" that are suggested. Are they true? If so, how can they be used to avoid bad relationships and build good ones? If you like, have your students form gender-mixed groups and discuss each axiom. Then they can report back to the class. This is sure to start off the chapter in a lively manner.
    - If it is the right relationship, it will work; if it doesn't work, it isn't the right relationship.
    - Every bad relationship has warning signs.
    - Having no relationship is better than having a bad relationship.
    - Don't settle for less than you deserve.
    - Get it right the first time—divorce is hell.
    - You will have the best relationship when you don't need one—that is, when you are content with your own life, rather than searching for a relationship to fill a gap.
    - When it comes to partners in relationships, it is better for the other person to want you more than need to you, and it is better to want than to need the other person.

STEP II: Classroom Activities

a. Use the PowerPoint presentations in *Multimedia Manager 2007* to complement your mini lecture.

b. Expand on key lesson themes
- **Stereotypes**

    1. For an unusual exercise in cultural diversity, I suggest using one from Dr. Chante Cox of the Carnegie Mellon University Psychology Department regarding her list of well-known and little known negative stereotypes that African-Americans have about white Americans. Go over the list with your class. Everyone knows the negative stereotypes about African-Americans that white Americans sometimes have, but most white students have never heard the ones about themselves. In fact, they are often surprised to hear that there are any! As they hear what they are, they are typically puzzled and astonished. After a while, all they can do is laugh out loud: These stereotypes are not merely untrue; they are ridiculous. And that is precisely the point: *All* stereotypes are ridiculous.
    2. This exercise tends to come in under the student's radar, so to speak— it is not like the usual cultural diversity lessons they have had and may have grown tired of, and it tends to work well. It really does encourage students to seek greater diversity in their relationships.

c.   Group Activities

- Creating a Shared Living Contract

1. Begin by having students discuss their experiences living with roommates.
2. Next, split the class into small groups. Based on the concerns raised in discussion, have students write up a contract that might help them avoid roommate frustration in the future.
3. You may want to provide your students with a sample contract to use as a model. One such sample can be found at http://www.rentiowa.com/pdf/roomcon.pdf (requires Adobe Acrobat Reader).

d. Peer Leader Assistance

- Divide your class into small groups of the same gender. Set the context as dating and mating. Then, pose these questions, and have the groups report back. Complete the reporting on one question before posing the next:

    o What are your gripes about the opposite sex?
    o What is it about men/women that the opposite sex needs to understand?
    o What are the things about the opposite sex that you prize and appreciate?

Students typically get so excited that you have to work to maintain control and not have people speaking all at once. However, it's fun and informative for your students, and will lead you into a vigorous discussion about relationships, communication, and stereotypes.

The peer leader's role in this topic is very important; students will want to hear how the peer leader has handled some of the issues that are being discussed or what advice he or she has to offer. Peer leaders can offer responses to several of the questions and pointers that are in the chapter margins providing that they feel comfortable to do so.

e. Case Studies

Professor Jones, Heather, and Sue

Professor Jones had the students in his first-year seminar write journals every week. Each week, he could expect some of the journals to be routine, some exciting, some happy, some discouraged, some funny, a few scary, and a few worrisome. This week, two young women's journals caused him some concern. Both women were eighteen years old and attending college for the first time. Neither was a very good student, but neither was failing, either. Heather seemed happy, cheerful, and energetic. She didn't make many contributions in class, but she was always present and loved talking to her fellow students before and after each class. Sue was much quieter. She sometimes missed class, but she was very apologetic when she did. In contrast to Heather's good cheer, Sue often had a certain look of sadness on her face, and she was much less outgoing with her classmates than Heather was. Sue usually did, however, manage to read her assignments and try to make some contributions to the class, although her confidence seemed a little shaky.

Here are the journal entries that caused Professor Jones to be concerned: Heather wrote, "I told him that I wanted to go out with him tonight, so he came and picked me up. We went and hung out at the fraternity house where I met all his friends; it was fun. It was soo wild! I saw more drugs, drinking, and fighting in one night than I have in three months. Every guy there was a complete scammer." A few days later, she wrote, "Tonight was soo much fun! All my friends came to the house to watch my brother's band play. We danced and drank and had a good time. It was completely wild! There were drug deals being made every time I turned around and people doing pot in the room I was in. There were a bunch of drunken jerks fighting about nothing and some guy cutting his wrists in front of everyone. Things like this just don't happen at home!"

Here is what Sue wrote in her journal: "I'm sitting in my dorm room by myself, thinking too much, as usual. I really need to be studying, but I just can't concentrate on school. It's weird how you don't think about something very often and then all of a sudden it hits you and then it's all you can think about. I miss my dad! It's been about nine years since he died and I can't believe how much of my life he's missed. The little girl I was when he died is barely the same woman I am now. Each day it gets harder to remember the way he looked in person or the way his voice sounded. I used to love to hear him laugh and now I can't even recall what his laugh sounded like. Maybe I'm thinking about him tonight because we had a parents' cookout this weekend. I loved having my mom and my stepdad there, but I would have given anything to have had my dad there. It's like he's half of me, and none of my friends will ever see where that half originated. I never got a chance to really know about him like I now know about my mom. You know as you get older, your parents start to share more about their past with you, and you can laugh and relate with them. But I didn't have that with my dad. Sometimes I do or say something and wonder if I got that from him. I hate nights like this. I miss him so much it literally hurts. When will I see him again? Will I ever see him again? The pain is unbearable."

Discussion Questions:
1. Do you think professor Jones should be worried about Heather and Sue?
2. Do you think either of them has a serious problem? If so, what is it?
3. What should professor Jones say to Heather and to Sue?
4. How could their parents approach them in a positive and helpful way?
5. If Heather and Sue were your roommates, what would you do or say? What can and should Heather and Sue do for themselves?
6. How do you think Heather and Sue probably fared in college and in their lives after they graduated—or do you think they probably would not make it through college?

f. Chapter Exercises

- **Exercise 13.1: Thinking about Friends**
  This exercise should be completed individually. Consider assigning it as an additional journal entry.

- **Exercise 13.2: Looking for Love**
  Have students complete this exercise in small discussion groups. It would work well when discussing boundaries in relationships.

- **Exercise 13.3: Balancing Relationships and College**
  Part A of this exercise can be turned into a group activity. The same can be said for Part B, but out of sensitivity to students' privacy, you may want to keep it as an additional journal entry.

- **Exercise 13.4: Student-Parent Gripes**
  We *highly* recommend this exercise. In the fall semester, we assign it just before Thanksgiving, which offers most students a good opportunity to discuss the Parent Gripes with their families.

- **Exercise 13.5: Roommate Gripes**
  This exercise helps students think about how they might pick a future roommate. If you use this exercise in class, you can be sure that many of the students will be experiencing some of the conflicts listed and will be eager to hear possible solutions.

STEP III: *Review and Preview*

REVIEW

a. Address Common Questions and Concerns of First-Year Students:

- *Why do professors think their dumb courses are the only things in our lives? Relationships and social activities are obviously more important to us, not to mention the jobs we have to work to pay the bills.*
  Answer: While student journals suggest that relationships take center stage with students, they must learn to balance college and work with their personal lives. Reminding them of their career and educational goals will help to reinforce this. Students need to be careful not to allow relationships to interfere with coursework and studying. Help them to learn how to develop healthy relationships.

- *Why is it so hard to find a decent man/woman? Why aren't there any good ones available? Why are men/women always playing games with you?*
  Answer: First of all, there *are* good men and women available. As the text states, it depends on where you "go fishing." Share with students that we often seek out partners based on initial attraction. Encourage them to take time to get to know people and not rush into a relationship. Long-lasting, healthy relationships are not based on sex or sexual attraction, but on other additional factors such as mutual respect, communication, and understanding.

- *How can I be expected to accept homosexuals when my religion condemns them and*

169

what they do is against the law?
Answer: Some people have this dilemma with homosexuality and their religious beliefs. Explain to students that although they may disagree with homosexuality, they can learn to accept the diversity of others. Professionals do not consider homosexuality a disease or mental disorder. This may be a good time to encourage students to practice tolerance.

- *Why are parents so impossible?*
Answer: For parents, as well as for students, this is often a time of great change. Although they may seem impossible, parents are usually genuine in their care and concern. They too are adjusting to your change in your going to college. There is no substitute for good communication skills if things are difficult between parents and students.

- *What can I do about my "roommate from hell?"*
Answer: Remember, roommates do not have to be best friends. This is a good time for students to practice good communication skills and learn how to compromise. Encourage students to seek help and try to work things out with their roommates. If they are having an extremely difficult time, they can ask their residence hall staff for assistance.

b. Writing Reflection

- To get the students to share thoughts about how relationships with parents have changed ask them to choose one or more of the six concerns/perceptions of parents mentioned on pp. 259-260 and, in a brief essay, justify or refute the perception(s) using critical thinking to defend their decisions.

PREVIEW FOR NEXT CLASS

Divide the class into groups of 4-6 and ask students to complete the assignment "Working Together: Reflections on Identity" on p. 288 for the next class.

E. Test Questions

Multiple Choice - choose ONE answer per question.

1. According to the text, one of the best things about going to college is
   a. meeting new friends.
   b. being on your own.
   c. finding a spouse.
   d. none of the above

2. Of the following, the only one you should become romantically involved with is
   a. your teacher.
   b. your boss.
   c. your co-worker.

d. It's not a good idea to become romantically involved with any of them.

3. If it is time to end a relationship, do it
    a. immediately.
    b. sternly.
    c. calmly and cleanly.
    d. All of the above

4. Relationships _____when they turn into long distance romances.
    a. flourish
    b. change significantly
    c. become problematic
    d. none of the above

5. Whether you live on-campus or at home, becoming a college student will
    a. not change your relationship with your parents.
    b. change your relationship with your parents.
    c. a & b
    d. none of the above

6. Greek organizations are
    a. a waste of time and money.
    b. a good way for students to "buy" their friends.
    c. philosophically distasteful.
    d. not all alike, nor are their members.

7. Being a college student can
    a. not coexist with marriage.
    b. not coexist with parenting.
    c. coexist with marriage and parenting.
    d. none of the above

8. A roommate should be
    a. your best friend.
    b. someone with whom you can share your living space comfortably.
    c. a & b
    d. none of the above

9. Electronic relationships can be
    a. fun and educational.
    b. transient and unpredictable.
    c. a & b
    d. none of the above

10. You can find out about campus organizations through
    a. activity fairs.
    b. printed guides.
    c. open houses.
    d. all of the above

True/False

11. Many 18- to 20-year-olds change their outlook and life goals drastically.

12. You should never maintain a long-distance relationship while in college.

13. In a recent study of college students, more than 50% reported they had ended a romantic relationship during their freshman year.

14. Never become romantically involved with your teacher.

15. The one sure way to have a good compatible roommate is to room with your best friend.

Short Answer

16. List four perceptions that parents have regarding their children who are in college.

17. Describe the steps a student should take if she/he is having roommate problems.

18. What is one major difference between a co-op program and a service learning opportunity?

19. What are two downsides of having an electronic relationship?

20. Name two advantages to having an on-campus job.

Essay

21. Consider and then summarize the likely benefits of service learning to the individual students who participate in it, to our educational system, and to our society as a whole.

22. It is easy to stay within our "comfort zone" by interacting mainly with people much like ourselves; why, then, are students (and citizens) urged to cultivate diversity in their relationships? What are the likely individual and societal benefits of doing so?

23. Describe the advantages and disadvantages in becoming part of a Greek club. How could joining a fraternity or sorority help or hurt you?

24. Describe and discuss key ways that you can insure that you live safely on campus.

25. Write an essay on the one major lesson you learned from this chapter.

CHAPTER 13 ANSWER KEY

1. a, p. 255
2. d, p. 258
3. c, p. 257
4. b, p. 256
5. b, p. 259
6. d, p. 263
7. c, p. 257
8. b, p. 261
9. b, p. 262
10. d, p. 263
11. true, p. 256
12. false, p. 257
13. false, p. 257
14. true, p. 258
15. false, p. 261

F. Web Resources

Dating Your Professor – http://www2.ucsc.edu/title9-sh/graduate/dating.htm
The University of California Santa Cruz offers a list of reasons why students should not get romantically involved with their professors or teaching assistants. You definitely will want to review your particular school's policy with your students during the course of this chapter.

"Breaking-Up" Is Hard to Do – http://www.counseling.ilstu.edu/DP/cope_breakup.shtml
This site, hosted by the Student Counseling Services at Illinois State University, offers advice for coping with the ending of a romantic relationship. It ends by suggesting that students who are having a particularly difficult time should make an appointment at a counseling center.

Electronic Relationship Advisor – http://www.pan-arts.com/era/
This site bills itself as "the Internet source for information, entertainment, resources, experiences, advice, and inspiration about on-line relationships." It features an electronic relationship addiction test, essays about electronic relationships, and "Tales from the (Internet Dating) Front."

http://college.lifetips.com/cat/59034/dating-relationships/

http://www.utexas.edu/student/cmhc/booklets/romrelations/romrelations.html

G. For More Information

Caron, Sandra L. (2002). *Sex matters for college students: Sex FAQ's in human sexuality.* Upper Saddle River, NJ: Prentice Hall.

Coburn, Karen Levin and Madge Lawrence Treeger. (2003). *Letting go: A parents' guide to understanding the college years (4th ed).* New York: Quill William Morrow.

Gray, John. (1993). *Men are from Mars, women are from Venus: A practical guide for improving communication and getting what you want in your relationships.* New York: HarperCollins.

Kaye, Cathryn Berger. (2003). *The complete guide to service learning: Proven, practical ways to engage students in civic responsibility, academic curriculum, and social action.* Minneapolis, MN: Free Spirit Press.

Seligman, Martin E. (1995). *What you can change and what you can't: The complete guide to successful self-improvement and learning to accept who you are.* New York: Ballantine Books.

Chapter 14: Diversity—Appreciating Differences among Us

Ideas for Instruction and Instructor Training	Videos and CD-ROMs	Media Resources for Instructors	Media Resources for Students
Instructor's Manual (IM) Includes a brief lesson plan for Chapter 14, chapter objectives, lecture launchers, commentary on exercises in the book, and case studies. **Test Bank (in IM)** Multiple Choice, True/False, Short Answer and Essay Questions. Also available in ExamView® electronic format, which can be customized to fit your needs.	***10 Things Every Student Needs to Succeed in College* Video** 6-minute segment entitled "Appreciate Diversity." **ExamView® CD-ROM** Computerized version of the Test Bank items for Chapter 14.	**JOININ™** Hand-held audience response device allows students immediate response to multiple-choice questions, polls, and interactive exercises. **Multimedia Manager 2007 CD-ROM** PowerPoint presentations, video clips, images, and web links help with assembly, editing, and presentation of multimedia lectures.	**iLrn® Pin-Coded Website** Contains self-assessments, electronic journals that encourage students to reflect on their progress, essay questions and exercises, and Test Your Knowledge interactive quizzes for Chapter 14. **InfoTrac® College Edition** May be bundled with text. *Keywords:* college success, liberal arts, goal setting, values, colleges, universities. **WebTutor™ Toolbox** Online course management tool for WebCT™ or Blackboard preloaded with text-specific content and media resources for Chapter 14.

A. Chapter Objectives

1. To provide basic knowledge and information about diversity in 20th Century America
2. To help students understand the concepts of culture, diversity, ethnicity and multiculturalism
3. To encourage an understanding of social change and the dynamic nature of diversity in America
4. To discuss the role colleges play in promoting diversity
5. To help students identify and cope with discrimination and prejudice on campus

B. Timing of Chapter Coverage

You may teach this chapter at any time during the term. It is probably best to give your students a chance to become acquainted with one another before discussing a topic as sensitive as this one.

C. About This Chapter

Teaching issues of diversity in any American classroom is very challenging. It's a subject of great intellectual depth, but there are also many emotional issues surrounding the topic. The trick is to teach the material in such a manner that the emotions become a part of the intellectual understanding students will develop. This is not easy and will require you to be in touch with your own emotions as you deal with this topic.

While the emphasis is on diversity in this chapter, it is as important to stress the dynamic nature of the issues. An emphasis on social change is critical. Students will benefit more if they come to an understanding that what they know, what they learn, and what they believe will be challenged by changes in all of the variables. It is the ability to recognize change and handle it in an appropriate manner that will be a major indicator of a well-educated person.

Diversity and Social Change

The assumptions underlying this chapter reflect the authors' experience of teaching this subject for many years, and the challenges of leading students to a "deep learning" of the issues. Some, but by no means all, of the assumptions of this chapter are:

- o Race is one of the most compelling ideas in American society. This is a long-standing situation, based on perceptions of complexion and other physical characteristics.
- o Students have very limited understanding of concepts of ethnicity.
- o Students have even less understanding of immigration and immigrant experiences. In some cases, recent immigrants may have been refugees who suffered painful experiences in reaching America.
- o Students have little notion of the dynamic nature of population composition and social change.

Contemporary students in American colleges and universities are much more diverse and complex than any groups of students in recent history. While we have a tendency to make generalizations about various groups, and students will often make generalizations about themselves, there is virtually no description that will be accurate or adequate for any one individual. The exercises in this chapter may be seen as challenging. The real challenge, however, is not in any particular exercise. The challenge facing us is that of creating a new world, a society in which the capacity to learn across social barriers will open extraordinary opportunities to every student.

D. Suggested Outline for Addressing Topics in Chapter 14

STEP I: BEGIN WITH A LECTURE LAUNCHER OR ICEBREAKER ACTIVITY
STEP II: EMPLOY A VARIETY OF CLASSROOM ACTIVITIES
    a. Use PowerPoint presentation from *Multimedia Manager 2007* resource
    b. Expand on key lesson themes
    c. Involve peer leaders
    d. Use chapter exercises
    e. Engage students in learning through case studies
STEP III: REVIEW & PREVIEW
    a. Address common questions and concerns about the topic
    b. Writing reflection
    c. Prepare for next class

Expanded Lesson Plan

STEP I: Lecture Launchers and Icebreakers

- In the last class, students were divided into groups of 4-6 and asked to complete "Working Together: Reflections on Identity" on p. 288 for the next class. Begin class with their responses to this activity. It will serve as a great lecture launcher.

STEP II: Classroom Activities

a. Use the PowerPoint presentations in *Multimedia Manager 2007* to complement your mini lecture.

b. Key Teaching Themes

The exercises that follow are challenging, some more than others. They are designed to push students beyond their perceived limits and lead them into deeper and more compelling learning experiences.

1. Every American comes to understand that people are treated differently based on their skin complexion. Have your students write a brief essay describing their memory of when they first realized people are treated differently because of their complexion. Ask them to describe what that experience meant to them or you could generate a classroom discussion on this topic.

2. Based on the data from the 2000 census of the American population, have your students analyze the racial and ethnic composition of their hometown, county, and state. They can do this by going to http://www.census.gov/ and selecting American Fact Finder. They can then follow the prompts to locate their home state, county, and city. Have them review the year 2000 data for each unit and write an essay on the racial and ethnic composition of each unit, making sure they discuss its significance in their lives. If possible, ask them to find similar data for the 1990 census and compare the two periods of time.

3. Assign students to construct a history of their family that starts with them at the center, and goes back as many generations as possible. Using interviews with parents, grandparents, and other relatives, as well as family documents and other resources, ask them to construct a history of race, ethnicity, and national origin in their family. Ask them: "Based on your study, how would you describe yourself in terms of 1) national origin, 2) ethnicity, 3) and race?"

c. Group Activities

- Assign students into small groups of three or four. Have your students learn more about the experience of slavery directly from those who went through that era. Ask them to log on to the Internet at http://memory.loc.gov/ammem/snhtml/ and go to the narratives of former slaves. Have them select two men and two women and read their accounts. Then, ask them to describe for the class their own perceptions of the experience of slavery based on these accounts.

d. Peer Leader Assistance

- Plan a field trip to the cafeteria or food court. Have students analyze patterns of social affiliation during the lunchtime hours (usually 11:00 a.m. to 1:00 p.m.) Ask them to observe where people sit, with whom they sit, and their patterns of interaction. See if they can identify those sections of the cafeteria often occupied by different social groups (athletes, fraternities, sororities, commuters, international students, minority students, and others). Have them write an essay on at least two of these groups on the subject, "Why (group A) and (group B) always sit together for lunch."

e. Case Studies

Renee

Renee's English teacher stops her at the end of class and asks if they can set up a meeting. Naturally, Renee is a bit apprehensive; most student-teacher conferences seem to focus on problems. But when she arrives for the meeting, Renee is pleasantly surprised—at first. Her teacher says, "I just wanted to compliment you on your writing skills. You are doing beautifully in my class…." Renee is about to thank her teacher when she hears the next words: "….for an African-American student." Renee is stunned and speechless. She doesn't know what to say. She gets up, turns, and walks out the door without saying anything. Her eyes become teary as she quickly moves toward the door of the building and heads for her next class.

Discussion Questions:
1. Why do you think Renee's teacher would say something like that?
2. Was Renee overreacting to the statement? Explain your answer.
3. Did Renee do the right thing by walking out of the office without saying a word? What else could/should she have done to explain her feelings?
4. Was there a lesson for the teacher here? If so, what was it and how could Renee help her understand it?

Professor Harris, James, Christina, and Ty

In a college success course, Professor Harris announces that two members of the Gay and Lesbian Student Association will be visiting class at the next meeting. One student, James, says, "What are they going to do, try and convert us?" Another, Christina, says, "It's against my religion." Ty chimes in, "I refuse to be in the same room with them." The other students simply sit there and stare at one another.

Discussion Questions:
1. Should Professor Harris abort the plan to invite the students? Explain.

2. Should Professor Harris explain why it's important to invite the students? How would she justify this?
3. Apart from the statements made by James, Christina, and Ty, what do you think was going on in the minds of most students in this class when Professor Harris made the announcement? What would you say made them think or feel this way?
4. How would you react if you were in the class? Explain.

f. Chapter Exercises

- **Exercise 14.1: Looking at the Curriculum**
  Place students into small groups and ask them to discuss the issues raised by this exercise.

- **Exercise 14.2: Diversity on Your Campus**
  After students complete this exercise, have them report their findings as well as what they found personally interesting to the class.

- **Exercise 14.3: Appreciating Your Gender**
  This exercise in identifying individual and group similarities and differences will help students learn to find common ground. Be sure to encourage tolerance and respect.

STEP III: Review and Preview

REVIEW

a. Address Common Questions and Concerns of First-Year Students:

- *I'm afraid I'll say something that will offend someone of another race.*
  Answer: It will happen, and sometimes you may not even know it. Use common sense and work on building a relationship with someone you like. Don't go out of your way to be friendly with other minority students if you really have little in common with them. Ask yourself, "Would I be friends with this person if he or she were from the same culture as I am?"

- *I don't think I'm part of any cultural group.*
  Answer: Everyone is part of some cultural group. It might be interesting to ask members of your family where your ancestors came from. You may discover that, rather than being part of one group exclusively, you are actually a mixture of several.

- *Is it okay to refer to people by race?*
  Answer: People from different countries usually categorize themselves by their homelands, not by race. Words such as "black" and "negro," used at various times in our history, have given way to the concept of "African-American," which more closely defines a group of people by its place of origin. As you well know, some "black" students

are not very black at all, and the word "negro" is considered a demeaning term used in the last century and earlier.

- *Are students of one culture naturally smarter than students of another?*
Answer: Not at all! You will find students of above-average intelligence in all cultural groups, just as you will find students who are average or below average. Because African-Americans were deprived for years of schooling comparable to their white counterparts, many thought they were not capable of learning. Few, if any, believe that today.

- *I get nervous when someone of my sex starts acting in a way that makes me think he or she is gay. I'm not gay and I don't want to be involved with gay people.*
Answer. Gays and lesbians make up around 10% of the population, according to some estimates. So it's almost impossible to isolate yourself from this group. Gays and lesbians are the last group to "come out" and defend their right to enjoy all of the opportunities and privileges of the straight majority. Remember, most gays and lesbians won't be interested in you sexually. Are you madly in love with everyone of the opposite sex you meet? We hope not.

- *Older students are threatening because they are more serious about their studies and "raise the bar" in classes they attend. How can I survive with them in my classes?*
Answer: Think a moment about the added demands on older students that you don't have to concern yourself with: keeping house, earning a living, raising a family, caring for elders and children, and so forth. Sure, they're going to work hard; they've invested lots of time and energy into getting a college degree. Instead of feeling challenged by them, get to know them. You'll learn a lot.

b. Writing Reflection

- Choose one or more of the reflection questions on page 289 in the text and ask students to respond in writing.

PREVIEW FOR NEXT CLASS
Ask students to complete Exercise 15.1 before the next class.

E. Test Questions

Multiple Choice - choose ONE answer per question.

1. The notion of different cultures celebrating their own uniqueness as well as the general culture is known as
    a. the American "melting pot."
    b. diversity.
    c. cultural individualism.
    d. civil rights.

2. _____ are parts of culture.
   a. Traditions and foods
   b. Language and clothing styles
   c. Artistic expression and beliefs
   d. All of the above

3. The terms ethnicity and diversity
   a. mean the same thing.
   b. have different definitions.
   c. are used interchangeably.
   d. b & c

4. The national language of Brazil is
   a. Portuguese.
   b. Spanish.
   c. Brazilian.
   d. None of the above

5. Generally, ethnicity is a quality assigned to a specific group of people who are historically connected by
   1. biological foundations.
   2. language.
   3. common national origin.
   4. b & c

6. Race refers to _____ shared by groups of people.
   a. biological characteristics
   b. language
   c. country of origin
   d. blood lines

7. A person with black, tightly woven hair texture could be someone of _____ decent
   a. African
   b. Cuban
   c. Puerto Rican
   d. All of the above

8. Making assumptions about group identity based on traits can
   a. do more harm than good.
   b. do more good than harm.
   c. help children.
   d. none of the above

9. Desegregation of schools in the U.S occurred in the

181

a. 1850s
b. 1860s.
c. 1950s
d. 1960s

10. The initial purpose of historically black colleges was to teach
    a. white men who wanted to work with slaves.
    b. freed slaves to read and write.
    c. slaves who escaped.
    d. none of the above

True/False

11. Women now outnumber men in college.

12. Colleges and universities are protected from acts of discrimination and prejudice.

13. On today's university campuses, the percentage students of color is less than the general population.

14. Acts of discrimination and prejudice often arise out of hatred for other groups.

15. Not every Latino speaks Spanish.

Short Answer

16. The term _____ refers to a group of people who are distinct from other people in terms of certain inherited characteristics.

17. The term _____ can refer to people of different races, or to people of the same race who can be distinguished by language, national origin, religious traditions, and so on.

18. The term _____ refers to the material and nonmaterial products that people in a society create or acquire from other societies and pass on to future generations. This includes beliefs, values, norms, and language.

19. List three ways we acquire our biases and beliefs.

20. List three ways in which colleges and universities can promote multiculturalism in higher education.

Essay

21. Do you believe colleges and universities should play an active role in educating students about diversity? Why or why not?

22. How does the information in this chapter differ from what you previously heard about race, culture, and ethnicity?

23. What do you feel are the benefits of living in a diverse society? How do these benefits directly apply to your life?

24. Write a community covenant or university creed that protects students from discrimination, prejudice, and insensitivity on your university campus. Develop a plan of action that could result in your university making this creed or covenant an institutional policy.

25. Why and how does diversity enrich us all?

CHAPTER 14 ANSWER KEY

1. c, p. 274
2. d, p. 277
3. d, p. 276
4. a, p. 276
5. d, p. 276
6. d, p. 277
7. d, p. 277
8. a, p. 277
9. c, p. 278
10. b, p. 278
11. true, p. 278
12. false, p. 283
13. true, p. 279
14. true, p. 283
15. true, p. 276
16. race, p. 277
17. ethnic group, p. 276
18. culture, p. 277

F. Web Resources

Diversity Database – http://www.inform.umd.edu/EdRes/Topic/Diversity/
Maintained by the University of Maryland, this database contains links to everything from a "Diversity Dictionary" to issue-specific sources, such as background information on various race and ethnicities.

The Case for Diversity – http://www.diversityresources.com/rc21d/menu_casefordiversity.html
This site offers more links, this time focusing on demographics. This is a wonderful resource that can be used with many of the Additional Exercises.

Race and Campus Climate – http://www.diversityweb.org/Digest/Sm97/eloquently.html
Written by Mary K. Rouse, Dean of Students, and Roger Howard, Associate Dean of Students, at the University of Wisconsin–Madison, this essay explores the racial climate on their campus, and how it has changed over time.

The Prejudice Institute – http://www.prejudiceinstitute.org/
The Prejudice Institute bills itself as "a resource for activists, lawyers, and social scientists … devoted to policy research and education on all dimensions of prejudice, discrimination, and ethnoviolence." It features free fact sheets about topics relating to prejudice, as well as an article examining the sociopolitical conditions in America post-September 11th.

Tolerance.org – http://www.tolerance.org/hidden_bias/
Created by psychologists at Harvard and the University of Washington, this site offers several tests that assess the "hidden" prejudices and biases we all have. Each test offers a tutorial that teaches users about the science behind the tests, stereotypes and prejudice, and the societal effects of bias.

Understanding Stereotypes – http://school.discovery.com/lessonplans/programs/stereotypes/
Although this lesson plan is geared toward high school students, it is easily adapted to the college classroom. The included web links – historical timelines for various ethnic groups, and several pages on tolerance – should prove useful as well.

How Race Is Lived in America – http://www.nytimes.com/library/national/race/
This series of articles by The *New York Times* is based on the premise that race relations are being defined less by political action than by daily experience. It includes archival articles and a list of resources found on the Internet. Free registration is required.

More Helpful Links:

http://curry.edschool.virginia.edu/go/multicultural/ - A Multicultural Pavilion offering resources and dialog about multicultural issues.
http://sln.fi.edu/tfi/hotlists/blackhistory.html - 27 links to black history websites.
http://www.columbia.edu/cu/lweb/indiv/southasia/cuvl/ - South Asia Resource Access provides links to Asian interest websites.
http://www.chcp.org/ - Chinese historical and cultural project which promotes Chinese American culture.
http://hirsch.cosy.sbg.ac.at/www-virtual-library_culture.html - Various links to different cultural websites

G. For More Information

Bonilla-Silva, Eduardo. (2003). *Racism without racists: Color-blind racism and the persistence of racial inequality in the United States.* Lanham, MD: Rowman & Littlefield.

Griffin, John Howard. (1996). *Black like me.* New York: Signet Classics.

Hollinger, David A. (2000). *Postethnic America: Beyond multiculturalism.* New York: Basic Books.

Marcus, Eric. (1999). *Is it a choice – revised edition: Answers to 300 of the most frequently asked questions about gays and lesbians.* San Francisco, CA: Harper San Francisco.

Von Loewe Kreuter, Gretchen. (1996). *Forgotten promise: Race and gender wars on a small college campus.* New York: Knopf.

Chapter 15: Exploring Your Values

Ideas for Instruction and Instructor Training	Videos and CD-ROMs	Media Resources for Instructors	Media Resources for Students
Instructor's Manual (IM) Includes a brief lesson plan for Chapter 15, chapter objectives, lecture launchers, commentary on exercises in the book, and case studies. **Test Bank (in IM)** Multiple Choice, True/False, Short Answer and Essay Questions. Also available in ExamView® electronic format, which can be customized to fit your needs.	**ExamView® CD-ROM** Computerized version of the Test Bank items for Chapter 15.	**JOININ™** Hand-held audience response device allows students immediate response to multiple-choice questions, polls, and interactive exercises. **Multimedia Manager 2007 CD-ROM** PowerPoint presentations, video clips, images, and web links help with assembly, editing, and presentation of multimedia lectures.	**iLrn® Pin-Coded Website** Contains self-assessments, electronic journals that encourage students to reflect on their progress, essay questions and exercises, and Test Your Knowledge interactive quizzes for Chapter 15. **InfoTrac® College Edition** May be bundled with text. *Keywords:* college success, liberal arts, goal setting, values, colleges, universities. **WebTutor™ Toolbox** Online course management tool for WebCT™ or Blackboard preloaded with text-specific content and media resources for Chapter 15.

A. Chapter Objectives

1. To learn some of the distinctions between types of values
2. To realize how societal values are in conflict
3. To illustrate how changes in American society have forced changes in societal values
4. To understand the difficulties in actualizing societal values
5. To discover how to put values to the test through service learning
6. To recognize that the way you manage your money relates to your values

B. Timing of Chapter Coverage

The subject matter of this chapter is such that you can teach it at any time during the semester. Reducing freshmen anxiety is very important in order to free their minds for other than strictly academic performance matters. This argues for delaying this chapter until they have understood the chapters devoted to subject matter mastery. On the other hand, Nevitt Sanford, perhaps the foremost scholar of college student development in the 20th Century, once said that the importance of a sense of community is that you can challenge students more in the context of a supportive community environment. This chapter will be more stimulating when there is an existing sense of community.

C. About This Chapter

The values literature is very frustrating for a number of reasons, foremost of which is the fact that authors who write about values use the term to convey different meanings in both the popular and the scientific literature. Therefore, in constructing definitions and exercises, we made a conscious choice to provide very specific definitions, tangible examples, and exercises where the student is in the role of investigator.

In the library, the usual search engines turned up thousands of largely non-comparable studies, a circumstance we felt would overwhelm first year students (or their instructors trying to help them make sense of the disparate information). Even going to the dictionary did not prove to be very helpful. We compiled a table of dictionary definitions that we did not find helpful as a teaching tool. See Table 15.1.

The topic of moral values has been politicized: there is pressure on first year students to adopt the "right" moral values. One of the books in the bibliography makes this point, but does so in a manner that can be very helpful as a teaching tool: *American Values: Opposing Viewpoints*. There are six chapter topics for this book, all with spirited excerpts:

1. What values should America uphold?
2. How are American values changing?
3. Is America in decline? (with specific readings by William Bennett "Moral Conduct is in Decline" and "Moral Conduct is Not in Decline" by Jeffrey W. Hayes and Seymour Martin Lipset)
4. How important are family values?
5. How do religious values influence America?
6. How does materialism affect America?

The point is that there are rich resources in the arena of moral values for stimulating assignments using the Web or examples from current events in the newspaper.

Our suggestions on teaching about intrinsic (ends) and instrumental (means) values involve using two tables from the pioneering research of Milton Rokeach (1973, 1979). He believed that there were finite lists of both ends values (he called them terminal values) and instrumental (means) values. He had different groups rank-order those values. The tables we provide show how two samples from the 1960s rank-ordered values (see Tables 15.2 and 15.3). Our suggestion is to have your students rank the same lists as they would do it and as their parents would do it. This will be a very rich exercise for discussion as there will be the two historical rankings by the Rokeach samples and current rankings.

Table 15.1
Definitions of "Values"

Definition	Source
Beliefs of a person or social group in which they have an emotional investment (either for or against something).	The DICT Development Group: www.dict.org/bin/Dict WordNet (r)1.6
Principles considered most important; moral codes.	Wordsmyth www.wordsmyth.net
The ideals, customs, institutions, etc., of a society toward which the people of the group have an affective regard. These values may be positive (cleanliness, freedom, or education), or negative (cruelty, crime or blasphemy).	Learning network/infoplease www.infoplease.com
Ideals, standards of a society	The Newbury House Online Dictionary nhd.heinle.com Heinle & Heinle Publs. © 1999 Monroe Allen Publishers, Inc.
Beliefs of a person or social group in which they have an emotional investment (either for or against something).	Ultra Lingua www.ultralingua.net/dictionary
Standards or qualities considered worthwhile and desirable.	Encarta Enquire ® Online concise Encarta.msn.com
Beliefs of a person or social group in which they have an emotional investment (with or against something).	Dictionary.com www.dictionary.com © 2001 Lexico LLC
The principles you have which control your behavior.	Cambridge Dictionaries Online Dictionary.cambridge.org © Cambridge University Press 2000
The principles or standards of a person or society, the personal or societal judgment of what is valuable and important in life.	Oxford English Dictionary © Oxford University Press 2001 dictionary.oed.com
Something (as a principle or quality) intrinsically valuable or desirable.	www.m-w.com © Merriam-Webster Inc. 2001

Table 15.2
Terminal Individual Values (Ends Values)
(Beliefs or conceptions about ultimate goals or desirable end-states of existence that are work striving for, Rokeach, 1979, p. 48)

Terminal Values (Rank order of importance by a national sample)	1968 (n=1409)	1971 (n=1430)
A comfortable life (A prosperous life)	9	13
An exciting life (A stimulating active life)	18	18
A sense of accomplishment (Lasting contribution)	10	11
A world at peace (Free of war and conflict)	1	1
A world of beauty (Beauty of nature and the arts)	15	15
Equality (Brotherhood, equal opportunity for all)	7	4
Family security (Taking care of loved ones)	2	2
Freedom (Independence, free choice)	3	3
Happiness (Contentedness)	4	6
Inner harmony (Freedom from inner conflict)	13	12
Mature love (Sexual and spiritual intimacy)	14	14
National security (Protection from attack)	12	8
Pleasure (An enjoyable, leisurely life)	17	16
Salvation (Saved, eternal life)	8	9
Self-respect (Self-esteem)	5	5
Social recognition (Respect, admiration)	16	17
True friendship (Close companionship)	11	10
Wisdom (A mature understanding of life)	6	7

(Adapted from Rokeach, 1979, p 133)

Table 15.3
Instrumental Values (Means Values)
(Beliefs or conceptions about desirable modes of behavior that are instrumental to the attainment of desirable end-states)

Instrumental Values (Rank order of importance by a national sample)	1968 (n=1409)	1971 (n=1430)
Ambitious (Hard-working, aspiring)	2	3
Broadminded (Open-minded)	5	5
Capable (Competent, effective)	9	9
Cheerful (Lighthearted, joyful)	12	13
Clean (Neat, tidy)	8	10
Courageous (Standing up for your beliefs)	6	6
Forgiving (Willing to pardon others)	4	4
Helpful (Working for the welfare of others)	7	7
Honest (Sincere, truthful)	1	1
Imaginative (Daring, creative)	18	18
Independent (Self-reliant, self-sufficient)	13	12
Intellectual (Intelligent, reflective)	15	15
Logical (Consistent, rational)	17	17
Loving (Affectionate, tender)	11	8
Obedient (Dutiful, respectful)	16	16
Polite (Courteous, well-mannered)	14	14
Responsible (Dependable, reliable)	3	2
Self-controlled (Restrained, self-disciplined)	10	11

(Adapted from Rokeach, 1979, pp. 133-134)

D. Suggested Outline for Addressing Topics in Chapter 15

STEP I: BEGIN WITH A LECTURE LAUNCHER OR ICEBREAKER ACTIVITY
STEP II: EMPLOY A VARIETY OF CLASSROOM ACTIVITIES
     a. Use PowerPoint presentation from *Multimedia Manager 2007* resource
     b. Expand on key lesson themes
     c. Involve peer leaders
     d. Use chapter exercises
     e. Engage students in learning through case studies
STEP III: REVIEW & PREVIEW
     a. Address common questions and concerns about the topic
     b. Writing reflection
     c. Prepare for next class

Expanded Lesson Plan

STEP I: Lecture Launchers and Icebreakers

- Students often think that they know exactly what their values are. Since they were asked to complete Exercise 15.1, have them pair up and share their lists. Tell them to note any differences in their lists. You can then ask for partners to volunteer to share their lists along with differences and similarities. This can be an excellent starting point for introducing some of the main concepts of this chapter, such as the different usages of the term "value," definition of a value, types of values, and conflicts in societal and personal values.

- The concept of value dualisms can be explored in the campus culture, especially when the domains of moral, aesthetic, performance, intrinsic, and instrumental are used. Introduce some of Lynd's other value dualisms to the class. There are twenty identified in the original text. Based on an informal survey of this current college population, students' personal value aspirations are fundamentally challenged by the following from Lynd (1939):

  - Everyone should try to be successful, **but the kind of person you are is more important than how successful you are.**
  - The family is our basic institution and the sacred core of our national life, **but business is our most important institution, and since national welfare depends upon it, other institutions must conform to its needs.**
  - Religion and "the finer things in life" are our ultimate values and the things all of us are really working for, **but a man owes it to himself and to his family to make as much money as he can.**

      o Honesty is the best policy, **but business is business, and a businessman would be a fool if he didn't cover his hand.**

Students' reactions to these dualisms should spark a lively class discussion.

STEP II: Classroom Activities

a. Use the PowerPoint presentations in *Multimedia Manager 2007* to complement your mini lecture.

b. Key Teaching Themes

- **Take a Value Stand**
  This exercise is designed to help students learn how to disagree, or agree to disagree and to show students how to open their minds to an opposing point of view.

Suggestions:

1. The time required is about one hour. The setting required is an open room large enough to hold the class (unobstructed by tables and chairs). The instructor uses masking tape on the floor (or posts signs on three of the walls) to designate areas for students to stand if they Agree (A), are Uncertain/Unclear(U) or Disagree (D).

2. Participants may stand anywhere in the beginning. Ask them to move towards **A, U,** or **D** in response to the statements that the facilitator will read. They have no option but to take a stand. If they are uncertain, they may stand in the center, but in doing so, they are committing themselves to explain why. Several issues are grouped and discussion doesn't need to take place until the entire group of issues is read. For example, read all of #1s lines before asking for feedback and ask participants to change their positions as the statement is altered. At this point the facilitator will ask the participants to sit and will request that they explain their point-of-view.

3. Because of time, choose only those statements that are relevant to the demographics of the class. You may want to add some new ones that include current events and news headlines.

4. After a statement is read, give students 30-45 seconds to decide which section best fits their response. The leader can then give the signal for everyone to move to the section they chose. This encourages students to think on their own and minimize peer pressure ("Where are my friends standing?").

5. Remember, this is not a debate exercise! Some folk are tempted to give a feedback rebuttal after someone has expressed an opinion different than their own. Try to avoid

this. A good way of avoiding a rebuttal-debate is by allowing a person to speak only once per issue.

6. Some people are more quiet than others and vice versa. The more vocal people tend to always voice their opinions. While this is the way most classes run, it is imperative that in "Take a Value Stand," the more quiet folk get their opinions heard. To encourage these folk, try saying, "Let's hear from someone we haven't heard from yet." This usually works like a charm. If it doesn't, pick someone.

7. With people who haven't been in a situation where their views are directly challenged, there is a tendency to avoid making decisions. As a result, a group of people may insist on sitting in the Uncertain/Undecided area. A good trick is to make it a rule that all those who chose to stand in the middle MUST voice their opinions. In doing this, the quiet ones that chose to stand there know they will be picked on and will prepare themselves.

8. "Take a Value Stand" is about differences, and history has shown us that differences and the ignorance of the "other" are what people fear the most. Because of this, opinions are sometimes met with tension and friction, especially when people begin to make whispered comments while others are talking, or make shocked remarks at someone's opinion. How you handle this is up to you, but it is imperative that you deal with it. Be prepared for it to come up.

9. Different people define the statements differently. Try to avoid defining it for them. For example, in the statement, "Women make good secretaries on committees," avoid defining whether you mean "only women" or "all women" or "women but not men" ...etc. Let them work it out.

The Statements

1. I believe in the commandment "Thou shalt not kill."
   - ❏ I would <u>not</u> kill in defense of my country.
   - ❏ I would <u>not</u> kill in defense of my family.
   - ❏ I would <u>not</u> kill in defense of my own life.

2. I do not believe in euthanasia (mercy killing). I would not pull the plug on the machine keeping my great grandmother of 96 years of age alive if she had a terminal disease and was in pain.
   - ❏ if she asked me to.
   - ❏ if she asked me to three times.
   - ❏ if she asked me to every time I visited her.

3. When a friend is doing something illegal or dangerous to himself or herself and it makes me feel uncomfortable, I would
   - ❏ shrug it off and do nothing.
   - ❏ joke about it.

    ❑ ask him or her to stop.
    ❑ get mad at him or her.
    ❑ just leave.

4. I believe that athletes who have contracted HIV/AIDS should be barred from playing contact sports.

5. If I were assigned a roommate who was HIV-positive, I would ask for a roommate change.

6. I believe that women should be permitted
    ❑ to serve in the military.
    ❑ to serve as pilots, naval officers, and support staff to front line roles.
    ❑ to serve in combat roles.

7. I believe that gays and lesbians should be permitted to serve openly in the armed services.

8. I believe that if a close friend of long standing confided in me that she or he was homosexual, it would not affect our friendship.

9. It is okay with my parents for people of different races (including you) to
    ❑ date occasionally.
    ❑ have a steady relationship.
    ❑ get married.

10. When it comes to relationships, the opposite sex thinks only about sex.

11. For women, money is an extremely important thing when they are looking for a relationship.

12. Birth control is the woman's responsibility.

13. It is okay for a woman to initiate sexual activity during a date. A woman can be bold and up front about her sexual needs.

14. Initially, I am attracted to someone because of his or her personality.

15. I would date someone who had a terrific personality but who was obese.

16. It is okay and appropriate for a woman to call a man for a date.

17. I would date someone who has a terrific personality but is physically disabled.

18. Women who initiate a dating relationship tend to be overbearing.

19. After a break-up, the two people involved can remain friends.

20. Women are more sensitive than men.

21. Single parents should be able to adopt.

22. Homosexuality is wrong.

23. Gay couples should be permitted to adopt children.

24. Women should have the ultimate decision-making responsibility with respect to whether to have the child or have an abortion.

25. Sex before marriage is wrong.

26. It is okay and in fact expected that men will sleep around.

27. A woman who sleeps with two different men is sleazy.

28. I believe in not using racial slurs.

29. I see nothing wrong with telling or laughing at ethnic jokes.

30. A person's religion is his or her own business, and a person is free to believe whatever he or she wants as long as it does not infringe on other people's rights.

31. I would date people who are of a different religion than I am.

32. We are all created equal. The color of a person's skin should not affect how people are treated.

33. When I come in contact with a large number of people from a different ethnic group, I become anxious.

34. When I hear the word "gang," I usually associate it with ethnic groups.

35. When I hear the term "terrorist," I usually associate it with Middle Easterners.

36. Bilingual education should be eliminated from public schools.

37. Able-bodied students should be given prior notice if their roommate is disabled.

38. It is harder to relate to someone who is physically disabled than to someone who is not.

39. Disabled students should have special priority for admission to college.

40. I would not have a problem if my R.A.
    o   was hearing impaired.
    o   was deaf.
    o   had a learning disability.
    o   had cerebral palsy.
    o   was mobility impaired.

41. Smoking dope should disqualify a candidate for consideration for a Supreme Court position or for the Presidency of the United States.

42. I believe the California coast should be opened to oil drilling.

43. Voter ballots should be printed in languages other than English.

44. The legal drinking age should be lowered to 18.

45. Flag burning should be illegal.

46. Grades are a fair indicator of
    o   who I am as a person.
    o   how much I learned in that class.

47. People who only belong to ethnic clubs or groups on campus limit themselves.

48. Affirmative action policies shouldn't have an effect on college admissions.

49. Students who are caught plagiarizing should be expelled, no questions asked.

50. Students should be allowed to date their professors.

Debriefing the "Take a Value Stand" Exercise

Suggestions:
1. Debrief students in small groups or pairs.
2. Begin by asking for general feedback about the exercise.
3. Ask them the following specific questions:
    o   Were there any surprises?
    o   Did you find yourself making assumptions and stereotypes about a person on the other side before you heard what they had to say?
    o   Is this exercise designed for you to learn more about other people or yourself?

c. Group Activities
*   See the activity above.

d. Peer Leader Assistance

- See the activity above.

e. Case Studies

Jessamine

Jessamine has made new friends with a small group since coming to college. She is really getting to know them and even has class with a few of them. They have been spending time before class in the cafeteria and working together in the library. Jessamine likes them because they are good students, serious about their education, and really seem to support each other even through tough times. Recently, though, Jessamine started going out socially with a new group of friends. She finds that they are really into partying, both at clubs and at one friend's apartment. While she likes to party and dance, Jessamine is beginning to see a different side of her new friends. Lately, after their course work is done, all they want to do is drink until they puke. She has tried to suggest some other activities like going to the movies or attending an on-campus event, but no one seems interested.

Discussion Questions:
1. What suggestions do you have for Jessamine?
2. What values seem to be in conflict here?
3. What campus or societal value dualisms can you identify here?
4. How are Jessamine's values different from those of her friends?

Mitchell

Mitchell has recently started college after working and living at home for a year and a half. He just got a part-time job in a law firm to help pay for his extra expenses. Mitchell is doing clerical work, mostly filing and some courier tasks within the office building. The job has flexible hours and excellent pay. He seems to have found a good balance of work and school. After a couple of weeks on the job, the attorney who manages the office asks to speak to Mitchell. He tells Mitchell that he is doing an excellent job, but strongly suggests that Mitchell cut his hair a little shorter. Mitchell has been growing his shoulder-length hair for years and when he goes to work, he puts it in a neat ponytail. The lawyer also asks that Mitchell not wear his baggy cargo pants and oversized shirts to the office. Mitchell's clothes are always clean and he thought his dress was appropriate for the work setting. After all, he is hardly in the public eye for the firm.

Discussion Questions:
1. What should Mitchell do?
2. What values are in conflict here?
3. What institutional values can you identify in this situation?
4. What value dualisms are present here?
5. How can Mitchell approach the values conflict with his employer?

f. Chapter Exercises

- **Exercise 15.1: Evidence of Values**
  This exercise can help students begin to identify their core values and beliefs. Facilitate a class discussion on students' final results after they complete this exercise on their own.

- **Exercise 15.2: Friends and Values**
  Part A of this exercise should be completed out of class. After completing Part B in small groups, consider asking students to write a response to the question, "How is it possible to be friends with someone whose values differ greatly from your own?" They can do this as a short paper or an extra journal assignment.

- **Exercise 15.3: Your Values and Your Family's Values**
  This exercise should be completed out of class, if only to give students an opportunity to chew over their questions and perhaps consult their families for opinions.

- **Exercise 15.4: Assessing Your Financial Health**
  This is a great exercise to use near the beginning of the chapter. You may also want to integrate this exercise into coverage of material from other chapters.

- **Exercise 15.5: Creating a Monthly Budget**
  The purpose of this exercise is to start thinking about developing a budget. This exercise should be done outside of class due to the personal nature of spending and debt. This can be a difficult exercise so encourage your students to review how they have spent their money and to begin thinking ahead for the future. If they are able to look ahead toward expenditures like a spring trip or traveling abroad, they might be more motivated to follow a budget.

STEP III: Review and Preview

REVIEW

a. Address Common Questions and Concerns of First-Year Students:

- *Why is learning about values so important?*
  Answer: From the global, national, community, and individual perspectives, these are challenging and confusing times in American society. Help students understand that values are a central element in determining the purpose of their learning and the utilization of their knowledge (for instance, their career). An important outcome of college is that students will learn to identify the values that will enhance their lives.

- *Why do you say this literature on values is confusing?*
  Answer: There are two reasons. The first reason is that the term itself has so many different meanings when it is used in the popular literature that is difficult to understand

what an author or speaker is trying to say. This makes comparisons between articles, newspaper stories, or other media coverage problematic. The second reason is that scientists use the term at different levels of meaning. This means that one scientist may investigate different cultures from an anthropological viewpoint and measure values within a cross-cultural context, while a sociologist can look at societal values from a social-class perspective. The viewpoint to emphasize is the necessity to look beyond the words to discern someone's underlying meaning.

- *Why is such an emphasis placed in this chapter on societal values?*
Answer: The reason for this emphasis is that American society itself has changed dramatically over the past half-century, and changes in values have followed from those structural changes. Further, with the explosion of information technology and the effects of globalization, the pace of change will likely accelerate. The society as a whole and its basic institutions smuggle (try to impose in hidden or deceptive ways) values. Since those values are changing, it is even more difficult for students to define their most enduring values.

- *Why was the specific format for classifying values chosen for his chapter?*
Answer: The first reason is that moral values are central to the fabric of civil society. There is no way that a humane society can be constructed based on law alone. Moral values are also the crucible for significant family relationships where there are such shared obligations for mutual welfare. Aesthetic and performance values are hallmarks of individual difference. The college years are a time where the very institution of higher education challenges students to expand their horizons on both types of values. Instrumental and Intrinsic value categories are very credible contributions from the science of value research to understanding the functions of values in people's lives. It is also possible to compare these values across generations i.e. to understand the "generation gap." The vignette from actor Russell Crowe and his father emphasizes this gap.

- *What is the biggest pitfall college students face when dealing with "cash" money?*
Answer: Defining and limiting their spending money. Pizza, snacks, beverages, fast food, clothes—if you do not clearly define what you will spend your cash on, you will spend your cash on almost anything. This can have you running to the ATM machine and leave you broke before you know it.

- *What is the best advice you can give a student concerning credit cards?*
Answer: Obtain at the most only one (you may not need one at all, but statistically speaking, most students do get a credit card). Define specifically what you will use it for (i.e. clearly defined emergencies or only for specific goods). Always pay off the balance at the end of the month.

- *What is the best one thing I can do to better manage my money?*
Answer: Be informed! Read and talk to people who know how to do it. Your parents may be a very good resource. Also see the resources in this chapter.

- *This chapter seems to suggest that I try to put some money into a savings account every month. If I only have $20 a month to save, and I have college loans, what good will $20 a month do me?*

  The valuable part about saving $20 dollars a month is the habit that you have developed. This money management skill will provide you with much greater rewards as you use this discipline with the paycheck you receive when in the national work force.

b. Writing Reflection

- Have students complete one or more of the journal entries

PREVIEW FOR NEXT CLASS

Divide the class into small groups and ask them to complete the Shared Values exercise on page 311.

E. Test Questions

Multiple Choice - choose ONE answer per question.

1. Which of the following apply to the concept of values as defined by Shaver and Strong?
   a. Values are standards for judging worth.
   b. Values may be applied to judge "things" like people, objects, ideas, actions, and situations.
   c. Values may be used to make judgments about whether something is good, bad, or neutral.
   d. all of the above

2. Moral values
   a. justify our behavior toward others.
   b. should be imposed on others.
   c. are something everyone inherits from their parents.
   d. separate means from ends.

3. Aesthetic values
   a. justify our behavior toward others.
   b. apply to a broad set of judgments about beauty.
   c. refer to values on performing to a set standard.
   d. have a relationship to ethical standards.

4. Means values are to instrumental values as ends values are to
   a. performance values.
   b. external values.

    c. intrinsic values.

    d. societal values.

5. Value dualisms
    a. are only formed in childhood.
    b. are easily recognized.
    c. are consistent across cultures.
    d. are conflicting beliefs.

6. The way you manage your financial resources relates to values and
    a. those of your family.
    b. credit rating.
    c. recurring monthly expenses such as phone charges.
    d. the amount of taxes taken out of your paycheck.

7. During the past decade, credit card companies have
    a. become an ineffective way of establishing a credit history.
    b. decreased their marketing to college students.
    c. increased their marketing to college students.
    d. suckered hundreds of thousands of college students into debt.

8. When accepting a credit card offer, you should consider all of the following EXCEPT
    a. how the interest rate is calculated.
    b. the consequences of not paying the balance in full each month.
    c. the color of the card.
    d. the minimum monthly payment, since you will always pay the balance in full.

9. A good rule of thumb is to not have more credit available to you than you can pay off in
    a. one month.
    b. two months.
    c. three months.
    d. none of the above

10. Which is NOT sound advice regarding financial aid?
    a. File for financial aid every other year
    b. Ask for a reassessment
    c. Meet all filing deadline dates
    d. Inquire every year about *criteria-based aid*

True/False

11. The word "values" has a definitive meaning.

12. Local values are always compatible with those held at the state and national levels.

13. Service learning is the same thing as community service.

14. Not every student is eligible for financial aid.

15. Fixed expenses are predetermined, recurring expenses, such as rent.

Short Answer

16. Give an example of a moral value, an aesthetic value, and a performance value.

17. Give two examples of value dualisms.

18. Define the following terms: *finance charge, grace period, late fee*.

19. What's a simple way to help protect your credit card?

20. Why should you always try to pay above the minimum required payment on your credit card?

Essay

21. Imagine you are a parent. How would you plan to teach your child healthy money management skills? Describe specific lessons you would teach and specific ages you would teach these lessons. Topics should include, but not be limited to, allowance, work, checkbooks, bills, savings, and credit cards.

22. Analyze how the media affect college students' spending habits and attitudes towards money.

23. Describe the three components of service learning.

24. What do you consider to be the most difficult "smuggled values" issues to confront for your generation of first-year college students?

25. Drawing on the insights from Robert S. Lynd, Alan Wolfe, and Derek Bok, what legacy do you want your generation to leave in terms of better actualizing society's values?

CHAPTER 15 ANSWER KEY
1. a., p. 296
2. a, p. 297
3. b, p. 297
4. c, p. 298
5. d, p. 299
6. a, p. 305
7. c, p. 307

8. c, p. 308
9. 9, p. 308
10. a, p. 306
11. false, p. 296
12. false, p. 300
13. false, p. 302
14. true, p. 306
15. true, p. 307

F. Web Resources

CollegeValues.org – http://www.collegevalues.org/
CollegeValues.org is a web site for the Journal of College and Character and the Character Clearinghouse published by the Center for the Study of College Student Values at Florida State University. It focuses on character development in college, as well as how colleges and universities influence—both intentionally and unintentionally—the moral and civic learning and behaviors of college students.

Ethics and International Affairs – http://www.cceia.org/
The Carnegie Council on Ethics and International Affairs is an independent, non-profit organization. It offers programs and publications that provoke thinking and dialogue about the urgent and complex ethical dilemmas involved in international decision making.

Personal Responsibility – http://www.heritage.org/Research/PoliticalPhilosophy/HL515.cfm
You can find this lecture on "The American Tradition of Personal Responsibility" on the website for The Heritage Foundation, a conservative organization. The essay, while pushing a specific agenda, raises several questions for your students to chew over while learning the material from this chapter.

National Service-Learning Clearinghouse – http://www.servicelearning.org/
This is the homepage of the Learn and Serve America National Service-Learning Clearinghouse (NSLC), which supports the service-learning community in higher education, kindergarten through grade twelve, community-based initiatives and tribal programs, as well as all others interested in strengthening schools and communities using service-learning techniques and methodologies.

Campus Compact – http://www.compact.org
Campus Compact is a national membership organization of college and university presidents committed to helping students develop the values and skills of citizenship through participating in public and community service.

G. For More Information

Bringle, Robert G, et al. (2003). *The measure of service learning: Research scales to assess student experiences*. Washington, D.C.: American Psychological Association.

Josephson, Michael S. and Wes Hanson, eds. (1998). *The power of character: Prominent Americans talk about life, family, work, values, and more*. San Francisco, CA: Jossey-Bass.

Lynd, Robert Staught and Helen M. Lynd. (1959). *Middletown: A study in modern American culture*. New York: Harvest Books.

Miller, John G. (1999). *Personal accountability: Powerful and practical ideas for you and your organization*. Denver, CO: Denver Press.

Mintz, Steven and Susan Kellogg. (1989). *Domestic revolutions: A social history of American family life*. New York: Free Press.

Chapter 16: Staying Healthy

Ideas for Instruction and Instructor Training	Videos and CD-ROMs	Media Resources for Instructors	Media Resources for Students
Instructor's Manual (IM) Includes a brief lesson plan for Chapter 16, chapter objectives, lecture launchers, commentary on exercises in the book, and case studies. **Test Bank (in IM)** Multiple Choice, True/False, Short Answer and Essay Questions. Also available in ExamView® electronic format, which can be customized to fit your needs.	**ExamView® CD-ROM** Computerized version of the Test Bank items for Chapter 16.	**JOININ™** Hand-held audience response device allows students immediate response to multiple-choice questions, polls, and interactive exercises. **Multimedia Manager 2007 CD-ROM** PowerPoint presentations, video clips, images, and web links help with assembly, editing, and presentation of multimedia lectures.	**iLrn® Pin-Coded Website** Contains self-assessments, electronic journals that encourage students to reflect on their progress, essay questions and exercises, and Test Your Knowledge interactive quizzes for Chapter 16. **InfoTrac® College Edition** May be bundled with text. *Keywords:* college success, liberal arts, goal setting, values, colleges, universities. **WebTutor™ Toolbox** Online course management tool for WebCT™ or Blackboard preloaded with text-specific content and media resources for Chapter 16.

A. Chapter Objectives

1. To recognize what triggers the stress response
2. To understand how to inoculate yourself against stress
3. To look at strategies for better nutrition and weight management
4. To discuss the many options you have for contraception and safer sex
5. To illustrate the science of alcohol intoxication and alcohol-related problems

B. Timing of Chapter Coverage

This chapter introduces students to survival skills that help them do well in school. These skills are developed over time and with exposure to challenges. Students may benefit from being introduced to these skills early in the term, but the material could be covered at any time. You may consider reviewing the section on campus crime earlier than you do the rest of this chapter.

C. About This Chapter

Stress

It is helpful for the instructor to mention some typical aspects of college life that students find stressful. They will come to understand that the stressors they feel are common and they are not alone in their struggle to handle them. The challenge is to get students to be introspective enough to recognize their own stress. Once this happens, strategies can be developed. Stress management is a personal behavior change. Research indicates that behavior change is very difficult for most people. Two elements seem to improve the rate of behavior change. First, people who develop an action plan with specific goals and specific actions that lead to the outcome seem to be more successful. Help the students to be specific with their action plans including active verbs, time frames, and evaluation. Second, people who incorporate the changes in their life plan are more successful with behavior change. Make sure the students understand that the way these pathways are established is through practice. Any behavior change when introduced into a life pattern seems awkward. It is not familiar and comfortable. But with practice it becomes normal. You could also encourage students to find a friend who is interested in behavior change and in teaming up to provide support for each other. For example, some students might want to initiate an aerobic exercise program. They could do this together and help each other stay committed to the plan. Some additional things to remember:

o Don't preach. Lead the students through discussion where they identify the important issues and questions.
o Set up a scavenger hunt and have students identify resources on campus that can help them with college stress. Do the same with resources for crime prevention.
o Teach students how to take their own pulse. They can use this information to determine if they are exercising aerobically.
o Demonstrate how exercise raises pulse rate by having the students take their pulse, do jumping jacks for three minutes, and then take their pulse again.
o Have students do an analysis of their diet, exercise, and caffeine intake.
o Record the relaxation technique in the book chapter and play it in class, play a professional tape, or have a counselor come to class and do one.

Sex

This section is not intended to be a comprehensive, in-depth unit on sexuality education. Chances are, students have been exposed to the basics of female and male anatomy, contraception, and STIs during their high school years. To present the material in this chapter, you do not have to be a "sex educator"! You do, however, have to be comfortable talking to others in groups about sexuality. At first, you may be uneasy and embarrassed saying certain words or discussing certain topics. This is perfectly normal. Getting that first word out may be the hardest. Take a deep breath and continue. It may be helpful if you openly admit to the class that you are a bit "nervous."

Establishing clear ground rules for class discussion may help diffuse discomfort. A good introductory class activity is to ask the class to brainstorm "rules" that will support a safe, non-threatening environment for everyone to participate. Examples of ground rules are:

o nothing that is said in class is to be repeated outside of class.
o refrain from laughing at or criticizing others' opinions.
o respect others' points of view.
o no talking while others are talking.

This activity can be conducted with the entire class as a large group or in pairs reporting back to the whole group. Visibly record the rules on the board and review them with the class. Ask a volunteer to copy the rules to notebook paper and then you can make copies and distribute them to the class at the next session. It may be helpful to refer students to the handout of "rules" before each class or on an as-needed basis.

One important reminder: As an instructor, your role in communicating key points from the chapter is not to judge, criticize or moralize. While you may have strong personal beliefs about sex, your role is to present factual information, help students clarify their own values, and facilitate responsible sexual decision-making, whatever your students' viewpoints and choices may be.

If you feel that you are unable or are too uncomfortable to review the content in this chapter, that's okay. Rather than skip the chapter all together, however, you may wish to access campus and community resources. Many colleges and universities have student health and wellness centers with trained staff whose responsibilities include speaking to classes, counseling students, working with faculty and staff, and preparing sex education materials. Ask colleagues or consult your campus and community phone directories for assistance in locating speakers and supplemental materials.

One of the challenges of teaching topics like sex that can stir emotions and trigger conflicting values, is knowing *how* to respond to student questions. When a student asks an awkward, embarrassing, or personal question or statement, *how* you answer is as important as *what* you answer. The following tips may help you:

- **Legitimize the question or statement.** Let the student know you have heard and understood: "That's a good question; lots of people ask/think/feel that."

- **Reactive positively.** No matter how shocking, unusual, or revealing the question or statement, the student needs to know you won't reject him/her. Look the student in the eye and smile: "I'm glad you asked/said that. I know it must be difficult to talk about this."

- **Be careful of your own negative feelings.** Don't let your own feelings interfere; a negative or fearful response will cut off communication. Keep your body language relaxed and avoid "put downs" (e.g., "You're too young to . . . " , "Where did you ever get that idea?!", etc.)

- **Don't laugh or make jokes about a student's question or viewpoint.** Many humorous questions are based on misperceptions or lack of information. *A serious question deserves a serious answer.* You might respond by saying: "A lot of people think that, but actually. . ."

- **If you are embarrassed, admit it!** Admit early on that you don't know all the answers and will follow-up on questions you can't answer; "That's a good question! I'd like to know myself. Suppose I find out and let you know tomorrow?"

- **If you can't answer or are uncomfortable answering a question, refer the student to someone who can.** "That's a good question; I wish I could answer but (give the reason). I'll help you find someone that can answer it."

- **Preserve the student's (and the class's) confidence.** While keeping personal information confidential is imperative, in certain instances, it may not be possible. Explain that you may have a legal responsibility to contact authorities and agencies (e.g., police, social services, campus security, etc.) if a situation warrants (e.g., rape, assault, stalking, etc.).

(Adapted from: Ponto, E. in Learning 87, Springhouse Corporation, 1111 Bethlehem Pike, Springhouse, PA 19477.)

Another point to keep in mind is that all of us are individuals with varying backgrounds and experiences that shape our values, beliefs, and behaviors. Effective teaching about sexual decisions or otherwise occurs when students are respected and their individuality acknowledged. Becoming aware of our own beliefs and assumptions about sexuality can have an impact on our teaching effectiveness. According to research, the following assumptions can inhibit student participation and learning:

- **All students come from "traditional" nuclear families.** Demographic trends clearly indicate this is not true. Today, there are more single parent, divorced, blended, and stepparent families than ever before. Moreover, some students may have grown-up in families with unmarried heterosexual or homosexual parents with adopted or foster children. Clarifying "family values" to understand sexual beliefs and behaviors cannot always be considered in traditional "mom and dad" terms.

- **All students are heterosexual.** While difficult to accurately measure, estimates suggest that 10% of students are *not* heterosexual. Some students may be questioning their sexuality and struggling with a variety of issues. Promoting inclusive and non-biased language (e.g., "partner" or "significant other") in instruction is crucial for creating a non-threatening trusting environment for sex education.

- **All students are sexually involved.** Many students are *not* sexually active and may need support for their decision. Presenting information in the third person as opposed to the second person ("you") will minimize judgmental perceptions and "preaching."

- **No students are sexually involved.** Denying that students are (and have been since whatever age) sexually active can also impact your effectiveness. Focusing on helping students clarify their values, improve decision-making skills, have healthy relationships, and seek resources is more important than determining students' sexual involvement status.

- **All students' sexual involvements are consensual.** Statistics indicate that many students from grade school to college age have been, or are being, forced to have sex. Not everyone chooses to be sexually active. This is particularly true in college populations where statistics indicate that 1 in 6 female students will be raped. Having referral information and resources available for your students, even if they don't ask for it, is necessary.

- **Students who are "sexually active" are having "intercourse."** Many people participate in behaviors other than traditional penile/vaginal intercourse. Even defining what constitutes "sex" and "intercourse" varies from person to person. For example, recent studies indicate that teens (and even adults!) do not view oral sex as "sex" and may engage in it as a "safer" alternative to penile/vaginal/anal intercourse. The point is: there are a whole range of behaviors—not just intercourse—that comprise healthy sexual expression and development.

(Adapted from: Krueger, M.M. (1993). Everyone is an exception: Assumptions to avoid in the sex education classroom. Family Life Educator, Fall 1993.)

A suggestion for teaching the information on alcohol is to use peer leaders to present the material and lead the discussion. These guest speakers are generally very well received. This gives students role models to question and follow. If peer leaders are not available, you need to be prepared to open and honestly answer questions about your own behavior, or at least be prepared to deal with questions about your behavior related to alcohol. Instructors can capitalize on the media and lead discussions about reports of incidents, often deaths, related to high-risk drinking among college students.

Understand what is really happening on your campus regarding alcohol use, alcohol policy, who enforces policy, and how they do it. You should also be well prepared to answer questions about local ordinances related to underage drinking, public drunkenness, DUI, and other alcohol-related offences. We strongly recommend that you contact the Office of Alcohol and Drug Programs and the many people on campus who are engaged in prevention and education related to college student drinking. The professionals can give you current information on behavior and policy. They may also be able to provide helpful materials.

Most of the exercises in this chapter are designed to encourage students to explore their own values. It is important for you or guest lecturers to avoid trying to impose values on others. Also, the journal entry (and exercise) topics for this chapter are extremely personal and private. Therefore, it may be inappropriate for you to collect and read students' writings or answers. Before making this chapter's assignments, always offer students a choice to submit or not to submit their work. Or, you may want to consider omitting this chapter's journal and exercises from course grade requirements all together. A visual check (without reading) of students who completed entries may be adequate toward participation points versus grade points. This approach may give students permission to honestly and openly complete the exercises or journaling activity on their own.

D. Suggested Outline for Addressing Topics in Chapter 16

> **STEP I:** BEGIN WITH A LECTURE LAUNCHER OR ICEBREAKER ACTIVITY
> **STEP II:** EMPLOY A VARIETY OF CLASSROOM ACTIVITIES
>   a. Use PowerPoint presentation from *Multimedia Manager 2007* resource
>   b. Expand on key lesson themes
>   c. Involve peer leaders
>   d. Use chapter exercises
>   e. Engage students in learning through case studies
> **STEP III**: REVIEW & PREVIEW
>   a. Address common questions and concerns about the topic
>   b. Writing reflection
>   c. Prepare for next class

Expanded Lesson Plan

STEP I: Lecture Launchers and Icebreakers

Ask students to give their definition of stress. After collecting several, introduce students to the physiological and psychological changes that occur when a person is stressed. Giving them a holistic picture of stress and the stress response will give them a clearer picture of how important it is for them to manage their own stress.

Invite a guest speaker to your class who can show your students some common techniques of self-defense. Perhaps your campus offers free classes on this topic and you can invite someone from a student life office or a counseling center. Arming students with tools to help them combat campus crime empowers them. It also helps make the theoretical chapter material feel more real.

STEP II: Classroom Activities

a. Use the PowerPoint presentations in *Multimedia Manager 2007* to complement your mini lecture.

b. Key Teaching Themes

- Sexual Readiness

    1. Divide the class into small groups of no more than five students. (It may be interesting to have gender separate groups to determine if there are differences in the results of the activity.) Explain that they will work in their small groups for 15-20 minutes and then report back to the class as a whole. Describe the following situation (you may want to prepare a handout with the following information on it):

You are hanging out talking with your younger 14-year-old cousin. Your cousin looks up to you and thinks that you have all the answers to everything, including sex. He/She tells you that he/she has been going out with a boyfriend or girlfriend and things are moving along. Your cousin confides that they will probably do it the next time they are together.

2. Ask each group to prepare answers to the following questions:

   o What will you tell your cousin?
   o What do you want your cousin to know about *before* he/she engages in a sexual relationship?
   o Make a list of ideas/topics you would cover with your cousin.

3. After giving the small groups time to brainstorm their ideas, ask a spokesperson to report their list to the class. When each group has reported their ideas, ask the class if they see any similarities across the lists. Differences? Are there gender differences based on the gender of the cousin selected and the group members? Do they feel that most 14-year-olds are receiving and considering advice that they would give? In closing, you may want to summarize factors involved in determining sexual readiness that the class brainstormed.

   (Adapted from: Fox, L.S. "Teaching the concept of sexual readiness" in Champeau, D. (1998). Great ideas in teaching health. Needham Heights, MA: Allyn & Bacon.)

- **Alcohol Use**

   1. Ask students to volunteer with a partner. Assign each team one of the situations listed below and ask them to develop a short role-play:

      o Dealing with a drunken peer who needs assistance
      o Confronting a friend whose alcohol use has created problems for them or others
      o Talking to their parents about alcohol use and information

   2. Give the students 10 to 15 minutes to prepare. Then, ask them to present their role-play for the class.

   3. Allow the class to process after each role-play is presented. Try to leave time for questions as well.

c. Group Activities

The objective of this activity is to give students more practice with relaxation techniques. This activity can be facilitated by the peer leader.

Suggestions:

1. Prepare students the day before by asking them to wear comfortable clothing. This is especially important if you decide the exercise is best served by having them lie on the floor. Make sure you arrange for some cushions or mats if you do so.

2. Read the following prompts to the class in a soothing voice to demonstrate how they can control anxieties by deliberately relaxing.

Settle back and get comfortable. Take a few moments to allow yourself to listen to your thoughts and to your body. If your thoughts get in the way of relaxing, imagine a blackboard in your mind and visualize yourself writing down all of your thoughts on the blackboard. Now put those thoughts aside for a while and know that you will be able to retrieve them later.

Now that you are ready to relax, begin by closing your eyes. Allow your breathing to become a little slower and a little deeper. Let your mind drift back into a tranquil, safe place that you have been in before. Try to recall everything that you could see, hear, and feel back there. Let those pleasant memories wash away any tension or discomfort.

To help yourself relax even further, take a brief journey through your body, allowing all of your muscles to become as comfortable and as relaxed as possible.

Begin by focusing on your feet up to your ankles, wiggling your feet or toes to help them to relax, then allowing that growing wave of relaxation to continue up into the muscles of the calves. As muscles relax, they stretch out and allow more blood to flow into them; therefore they gradually feel warmer and heavier.

Continue the process into the muscles of the thighs; gradually your legs should feel more and more comfortable and relaxed.

Then concentrate on all of the muscles up and down your spine, and feel the relaxation moving into your abdomen; as you do so you might also feel a pleasant sense of warmth moving out to every part of your body. Next, focus on the muscles of the chest. Each time you exhale, your chest muscles will relax just a little more. Let the feeling flow up into the muscles of the shoulders, washing away any tightness or tension, allowing the shoulder muscles to become loose and limp. And now the relaxation can seep out into the muscles of the arms and hands as they become heavy, limp, and warm.

Now move on to the muscles of the neck—front, sides, and back— imagining that your neck muscles are as floppy as a handful of rubber bands. And now relax the muscles of the face, letting the jaw, cheeks, and sides of the face hang loose and limp.

Now relax the eyes and the nose, the forehead and the scalp. Let any wrinkles just melt away. Now, taking a long, slow, deep breath, cleanse yourself of any remaining tension.

You might want to hand out copies to your students and suggest that they tape the script and play it back when they are in need of relaxation.

d. Peer Leader Assistance
See the exercise above.

e. Case Studies

Rory
Rory is a pre-med student. Both of her parents are physicians. Growing up, Rory never thought about being anything but a physician. She says she wants to be a physician but also feels a lot of pressure from her parents to be one. She is aware of how competitive it is to get into medical school, so she's very concerned about getting good grades. As midterms approach, Rory feels herself getting more and more stressed. She's having trouble sleeping, feels sick to her stomach, and has completely lost her appetite. She has also gotten into several arguments with her roommate lately. To avoid further conflict, Rory tries to spend as much time away from her room as possible, often studying at the library until closing and then moving into her dorm's lounge. She often doesn't get to bed until three or four in the morning, even though she has a Spanish class that meets every day at 9 a.m.

Discussion Questions:
1. What are some mistakes Rory is making in terms of dealing with her stress?
2. How could Rory better manage her stress?
3. Should Rory discuss her anxiety with her parents? What should she say?

James
James is on an academic scholarship that requires him to maintain a certain grade point average. He's had a rough semester and needs to do well on his finals in order to pull the grades that will keep him on scholarship. James is often tense regardless of exam schedules, but when he found out he would have three finals on the same day, he had a meltdown. First, he was angry that his schedule turned out this way and he has complained bitterly about it to anyone who would listen. Then he got into an argument with his roommate, who was listening to music while James was trying to study. The night before his exams, James studied at the library all night. He skipped breakfast the next morning because he wanted get to the classroom early. The teacher passed out the test and James began to read it. He felt absolute panic. All the typing on the page was running together, his vision was blurred, and he couldn't remember anything. The longer he sat there, the worse it got. Finally, he decided to guess on the questions and get out of the room as fast as he could. He was so upset, he skipped his next two finals as well. He spent the rest of the day hiding out in his bed, wondering what he was going to do and how he was going to tell his mother he failed out of school.

Discussion Questions:

1. Is there anything James could have done to handle this situation better?
2. What was the cause of tension between James and his roommate?
3. What are some test-taking strategies that would have helped him do better on the test?
4. Should James approach his teachers about what happened with his final exams? What would be the best way for him to do this?
5. If you were James's professor, how would you handle this situation?

f. Chapter Exercises

- **Exercise 16.1: Monitoring Your Stress**
  Have the students fill out this inventory at the beginning of this unit, or make it a take-home assignment. It's important for them to recognize their personal level of stress.

- **Exercise 16.2: The College Readjustment Rating Scale**
  This inventory may work better as a take-home assignment. You can ask students to volunteer sharing their reactions with the rest of the class, but due to the sensitive nature of some of the questions, it may not be a good idea to have them do so in required groups.

- **Exercise 16.3: Changing Perceptions**
  After the students have interviewed a person they think handles stress well, use that information to begin developing a list of potential strategies for managing stress.

- **Exercise 16.4: Doing a Weekly Check**
  This inventory may work better as a take-home assignment. You can ask students to volunteer sharing their reactions with the rest of the class.

- **Exercise 16.5: What's Your Decision?**
  This is a personal assignment.

- **Exercise 16.6: Quality of Life**
  This exercise can be done as an in-class assignment.

STEP III: *Review and Preview*

REVIEW

a. Address Common Questions and Concerns of First-Year Students:

- *How can I deal with the pressures of college? Sometimes I feel like I am going to explode.*
  Answer: Students need to know that this is a perfectly normal reaction. They also need to know it's something they can control. Emphasize to them that time management, stress

inoculation, and relaxation techniques can all help to reduce that "I am going to explode" feeling.

- ***Where can I go for help with stress management?***
  Answer: You may want to invite someone from your campus's counseling center to come speak to your students about their stress management resources. It's also a good idea to discuss other options, such as yoga/meditation classes.

- ***Will people think I am weak if I get help with stress management?***
  Answer: Some students may have a difficult time asking for help because to them it feels like admitting failure. They need to know that all college students feel overwhelmed and overstressed at certain times and that there is no shame in getting help.

- ***How do you find time to do stress management?***
  Answer: This is a common problem, and not only for students. Impress upon your class how important it is for them to schedule "me" time, whether it's to work out, prepare a healthy meal, get eight solid hours of sleep, or meditate.

- ***I think I may have a STI, but I'm not sure. What should I do?***
  Answer: It is important that students not ignore this thought or their health. If they think they have been exposed, they should go and see someone right away. Some options are community health centers, student health services, their doctor, or the local hospital. From there they can get guidance about what steps they need to take to help themselves both physically and emotionally.

- ***I had sex last night, but didn't mean to. What do I do now?***
  Answer: This is a potentially serious situation for many students. Sometimes sex happens in haste or ignorance and may leave a student emotionally scarred, exposed to STIs, or even pregnant. Encourage students to seek help right away from student health services, their doctor, community health services, and counseling centers. They should check out both their physical and emotional health.

- ***I am really uncomfortable with hearing and talking about this stuff in class and with members of the opposite sex present. Do I have to share my personal experiences and thoughts about sex or alcohol with my classmates or the teacher?***
  Answer: Some students will not be comfortable sharing their thoughts, experiences, or even opinions in class. It is important that you respect this and insist on mutual respect in the classroom. You will find enough students who do want to share so let them do so without putting the quieter students on the spot. Tell students it's okay to keep these matters private.

b. Writing Reflection

- The journal entry (and exercise) topics for this chapter are extremely personal and private. Therefore, it may be inappropriate for you to collect and read students' writings or answers.

E. Test Questions

Multiple Choice - choose ONE answer per question.

1. All of the following happen during the stress response EXCEPT
   a. an increase in heart rate.
   b. a decrease in stomach and intestinal functioning.
   c. an increase in the effectiveness of the immune system.
   d. a decrease in blood flow through arteries.

2. According to the College Readjustment Reading Scale, you have experienced a great deal of stress if your score is _____ or higher.
   a. 10
   b. 130
   c. 150
   d. 160

3. The best starting point for handling stress is to pay attention to
   a. diet and exercise.
   b. sleep and mental health.
   c. a & b
   d. none of the above

4. According to the text, _____ percent of adults do not get the recommended eight hours of sleep
   a. 53
   b. 63
   c. 73
   d. 83

5. According to the text, the average weight gain for men and women during the first year of college is
   a. 6 and 4.5 lbs.
   b. 7 and 8.5 lbs.
   c. 13 and 15 lbs.
   d. none of the above

6. Which is a sign of an eating disorder?
   a. Intense fear of gaining weight
   b. Stopping or never getting a monthly period

    c. Over exercising

    d. All of the above

7. For those who use smokeless tobacco, one "dip" delivers the same amount of nicotine as
    _____cigarettes

    a. 1 to 2

    b. 3 to 4

    c. 5 to 6

    d. None of the above

8. According to the text, the body usually gets rid of alcohol at the rate of

    a. 1 drink per hour.

    b. 2 drinks per hour.

    c. 3 drinks per hour.

    d. None of the above

9. Each year, _____college students between the ages of 18-24 die from alcohol-related
    injuries.

    a. 1200

    b. 1500

    c. 1600

    d. 1700

10. According to the text, which of the following contraceptive methods offers protection from
    STDs?

    a. Abstinence and cervical cap

    b. Condom and the Pill

    c. Diaphragm

    d. None of the above

True/False

11. STDs are only spread through genital contact.

12. You should aim for eight hours of sleep each night.

13. Caffeine consumption can impact your stress level.

14. Depression requires medical attention.

15. If you engage in heavy drinking for too long, your body can tolerate large amounts and you
    become an alcoholic.

Short Answer

16. Describe three things that happen in your body or mind during the stress response.

17. List three ways to inoculate stress.

18. What are the four techniques for managing stress?

19. Which contraceptive methods protect against HIV and STDs?

20. What are four signs and symptoms of someone with an eating disorder?

Essay

21. Discuss the relaxation techniques discussed in the text. What are they and how do they work? How do these techniques help the body deal with stress?

22. Both men and women may feel pressures to become sexually active or to increase their sexual activity. Explain two "encouragers" and two "discouragers" that may impact someone's decision to have sex. In your answer, be sure you clearly identify which is which and show how each contributes to a person's decision-making process.

23. Recently college presidents have identified alcohol use as the number one public health issue facing college students. Identify several guidelines that you follow to protect yourself from experiencing an alcohol related problem and being the victim of someone else's alcohol-related behavior.

24. What do you believe is the greatest single threat to your health, safety, and academic performance? Why?

25. Name the two major categories of reasons why students drink. What advice can you give them?

CHAPTER 17 ANSWER KEY
1. c, p. 317
2. c, p. 317
3. c, p. 317
4. b, p. 319
5. a, p. 323
6. d, p. 324
7. a, p. 334
8. a, p. 329
9. c, p. 330
10. d, p. 338
11. false, p. 326
12. true, p. 319

13. true p. 327
14. true, p. 320
15. true, p. 332

F. Web Resources

Coping with Everyday Problems – http://www.nmha.org/infoctr/factsheets/41.cfm
This fact sheet is from the National Mental Health Association. It defines what stress is, how to deal with it, and information about where to get help.

Stress Management – http://carlisle-www.army.mil/apfri/stress_management1.htm
From the Army Physical Fitness Research Institute, comes this in-depth source about stress and stress management. It includes information on diet and stress, exercise and stress, and more breathing techniques to reduce stress.

Stress Management Information Directory – http://www.stress—management.com/
This page offers a brief article, "How to Manage Stress at Work and Home," followed by an exhaustive list of web links to other Internet-based sources relating to stress and stress management.

Personal Safety Tips – http://www.elon.edu/safety/protect/safetips.htm
From Elon University, comes this great resource that helps arm students to protect themselves from campus crime.

Birth Control – http://www.plannedparenthood.org/bc/
This resource on birth control options is offered by Planned Parenthood, the world's largest and most trusted voluntary reproductive health care organization. It contains information about everything from abstinence to Depo-Provera (a.k.a. "the shot").

STI Online – http://sti.bmjjournals.com/
Sexually Transmitted Infections is the world's longest running international journal dealing with issues of sexual health and medicine. Each issue includes editorials, review articles, research methodology, clinicopathological conferences and correspondence.

Intimate Partner Violence – http://www.cdc.gov/ncipc/factsheets/ipvfacts.htm
This site, affiliated with the Centers for Disease Control, offers information about intimate partner violence—everything from statistics to a list of risk factors.

Binge Drinking Epidemic – http://www.health.org/govpubs/prevalert/v5/2.aspx
From the Substance Abuse and Mental Health Services Administration Center for Substance Abuse Prevention, comes this "Prevention Alert" about the growing problem of binge drinking on college campuses.

Facts about College Smoking – http://www.uri.edu/smokefree/facts.html
The University of Rhode Island hosts this page, which lists some startling facts about college-aged students and smoking.

G. For More Information

Benson, Herbert and Miriam Z. Klipper. (1976). *The relaxation response.* New York: HarperTorch.

Elkin, Allen. (1999). *Stress management for dummies.* New York: For Dummies.

Gaddes, Patricia. (2000). *Dangerous dating: Helping young women say no to abusive relationships.* New York: Shaw Books.

Gowen, L. Kris. (2003). *Making sexual decisions: The ultimate teen guide.* Lanham, MD: Rowman & Littlefield.

Handsfield, H. Hunter. (2000). *Color atlas and synopsis of sexually transmitted diseases.* New York: McGraw-Hill.

Trechsel, Jane Goad and Rodney Yee. (2002). *A morning cup of yoga: One simple, balanced routine for a lifetime of health & wellness.* Birmingham, AL: Crane Hill Publishers.

Wells, Donna Koren and Bruce C. Morris. (2000). *Keep safe!: 101 ways to enhance your safety and protect your family.* Eugene, OR: Harvest House.

Whitman, Neil A. et al. (2000). *Student stress: Effects and solutions.* San Francisco, CA: Jossey-Bass.